Millennium Madness

2,000 Ways to Mark the Moment

by Annemarie Marek and Debbie Berens

Annemarie & Debbie

Published by
MAREK & COMPANY/PUBLISHING DIVISION
6928 Cornelia Lane • Dallas, Texas 75214
Phone: 214/828-0634 • Fax: 214/828-4559

Website
2000ways2celebrate.com

ISBN 0-9674401-0-6 (pbk.)

First Printing * September 1999

Millennium Madness is available for special volume purchases for sales promotions, premiums, fundraising, or educational use. For details, contact the National Sales Director at 214/828-0634.

Printed in the USA by Morris Publishing
3212 East Highway 30 • Kearney, NE 68847 • 1-800-650-7888

A Note from the Authors

Some of the ideas in this book are wild. Some are wacky, and some are worthy.

We've come up with 2,000 ideas for you, but the possibilities are truly limitless. We hope you'll celebrate the new Millennium in a way that you'll always remember—simply, lavishly, or just plain low-key. Enjoy the moment and mark it with special memories!

P.S. It is mathematically correct that the new Millennium begins January 1, 2001. But who cares when everybody's partying in Year 2000? Enjoy the fun. Then, repeat it next year!

Special Thanks

It's not easy to invent 2,000 ideas to mark the Millennium. In fact, by the time we reached idea #1,876, we were stuck. How could we finish the book? We were short by 124 ideas. So we turned to our families, friends, nephews and nieces for their help.

A special thanks to Julie, Jim, Rosemary, Cameron, Christian, Catherine, Dana, John, Leslie, DeeAnne, and our Moms!

Now, we have something to share with you and celebrate!

Dedication

This book is dedicated to everybody.
Take time to celebrate.
You deserve it.

2,000 Anything! ❶

1. Make 2,000 wishes with 2,000 pennies in your favorite fountains.
2. Mail 2,000 certificates recognizing people who have made an impact on your life.
3. Pull out a road map and plot 2,000 miles in any direction, then load up your car and drive there to celebrate.
4. At midnight on the new M, ring every church bell a total of 2,000 times.
5. Send off 2,000 fireworks for every big celebration during the new M.
6. Distribute 2,000 ribbons to raise awareness of an important cause during the new M.
7. Send 2,000 packets of sugar to your "sugar."
8. Send 2,000 peanuts to your favorite "nut."
9. Ask 2,000 kids to draw pictures of what the new M means and publish them in your local paper.
10. Rent a limo and tour every street with a 2,000 block number in your community.
11. Fill your backyard with 2,000 balloons.
12. Fill your swimming pool with 2,000 balloons.
13. Run 2,000 yards in any direction just to see something new.
14. Hang 2,000 party streamers from your trees.
15. Start an e-mail chain letter to gather 2,000 signatures worldwide.
16. Sprinkle 2,000 rose petals on your front walkway (that's about 100 roses).

17. Invite 200 people to the beach and ask each to bring 10 tea lights.

18. Promise to spend 2,000 minutes (or less than 2 consecutive days) with your family to celebrate.

19. Give away 2,000 popsicles to school kids.

20. Put 2,000 "Happy M" miniature flags in 2,000 yards.

21. Decorate your house with 2,000 outdoor lights.

22. Buy 2,000 peanuts and take your family to the zoo.

23. Give away 2,000 smiles to friends and strangers.

24. Say "thank you" at least 2,000 times in the new M.

25. Ice down 2,000 beers from around the world and share them with your buddies!

26. Pass out 2,000 pieces of bubble gum.

27. Get your local radio station to play the top 2,000 hits of all time.

28. Give away 200 phone cards worth $10 in time.

29. Buy 2,000 small bags of M&Ms to celebrate. (Note: Two M's in Latin equals 2,000.)

30. Publish a booklet of 2,000 of your favorite sayings and give copies away.

31. Give away 2,000 fortune cookies.

32. Learn 2,000 things about other people and countries around the globe.

33. Write a list of 2,000 goals to achieve for the rest of your lifetime.

34. Build a castle with 2,000 popsicle sticks.

35. Build a tower with 2,000 sugar cubes.

36. Give 2,000 presents to 2,000 neighbors.

37. Climb 2,000 feet in a day.

38. Buy a house with 2,000 square feet.

39. Swim 2,000 laps.

40. Tell 2,000 jokes.

41. Send out 2,000 suckers.

42. Collect 2,000 golf balls.

43. Take mass transit to work for 2,000 days.

44. Print up 2,000 bumper stickers with your new M motto.

45. Create a trivia game with milestones of 2,000 anything.

46. Write a 2,000 word essay on what the new M means to you.

47. Send a 2,000 word letter to someone you've missed for years.

48. Eat 2,000 black eyed peas for good luck.

49. Do 2,000 reps of anything. Practice makes perfect.

50. Wind up 2,000 Baby Ben clocks and set them to go off at midnight December 31, 1999.

51. Learn 2,000 words in another language.

52. Travel 2,000 miles by air, water, or roadway.

53. Create a "connect-the-dots" picture with 2,000 points.

54. Solve a 2,000 piece puzzle with your friends.

55. Give away 2,000 miniature ceremonial flags.

56. Put 2,000 pinwheels in your yard on a breezy day.

57. Take 2,000 photos of everything you've always wanted to remember.

58. Tag team a cross country trip with your buddies and break the 2,000-mile barrier.

59. Sponsor a non-stop 2,000 minute poetry slam.

60. Create a book of 2,000 new M toasts.

61. Start to collect 2,000 of anything you've always loved.

62. Count 2,000 birds on the beach.

63. Read 2,000 pages of anything.

64. Sew 2,000 sequins on your new M power dress.

65. Read 2,000 poems during the year.

66. Fly 2,000 kites in an open field.

67. Release 2,000 birds in an open field.

68. Dare to make $2,000 more each year.

69. Save $2,000 to enjoy.

70. Take a $2,000 vacation.

71. Hug 2,000 people.

72. Give away 2,000 new M coasters.

73. Give away 2,000 new M posters.

74. Give away 2,000 new M t-shirts.

75. Create a path of 2,000 stepping stones.

76. Count 2,000 beautiful bodies on the beach.

77. Sail 2,000 miles in any direction.

78. Surf 2,000 waves in the new M.

79. Build a 2,000 foot-long sand castle.

80. Count 2,000 sea shells on the beach and save Number 2,000.

81. Clear out 2,000 things that clutter your life.

82. Give away 2,000 chocolate kisses to people you meet.

83. Light 2,000 candles in your driveway.

84. Take a 2,000 yard walk with someone you love.

85. Spare 2,000 seconds of silence to give thanks for your blessings.

86. String 2,000 paper clips together and wear it as a new M necklace.

87. Stretch a clothesline across your yard with 2,000 clothes pins and attach a special thought to each.

88. Release 2,000 helium balloons filled with new M messages.

89. Customize a batch of fortune cookies with special M messages.

90. Take 2,000 minutes of your time to write down your family's history.

91. Take 2,000 minutes of your time to dance.

92. Take 2,000 minutes of your time to learn a new language.

93. Take 2,000 minutes of your time to read.

94. Take 2,000 minutes of your time to play a musical instrument that you gave up long ago.

95. Take 2,000 minutes of your time to get back into shape.

96. Take 2,000 minutes of your time for random acts of kindness.

97. Take 2,000 minutes of your time to meditate.

98. Take 2,000 minutes of your time to learn something new.

99. Take 2,000 minutes of your time to breath fresh air.

100. Take 2,000 minutes of your time to get away from the city into the country.

101. Take 2,000 minutes of your time to explore a new place.

102. Take 2,000 minutes of your time to get back in touch with an old friend.

103. Print 2,000 cards with a special M greeting to pass out to everyone.

104. Choose any souvenir with the number 2000 on it and save it for yourself or your kids.

105. Send out 2,000 postcards of your favorite place—and be there for the new M!

106. Create a collection set of the best 2,000 songs of the past M.

107. Burn 2000 calories with your favorite exercise.

108. Go on a $2,000 fantasy window shopping spree.

109. Paint 2,000 on the four fingernails of each hand.

110. Make a 2,000 M bumper sticker that says: "I made it to the new M!"

111. Take 2,000 minutes of your time to relax in a hot tub.

112. Decorate your trees and shrubs with 2,000 miniature lights.

113. Take at least 2,000 minutes off during the new M.

114. Save 2,000 pennies every week (that's only $20).

115. Find 2000 images that reflect who you are, where you've been, and where you're going.

116. Celebrate your 2,000th week of being married.

117. Celebrate your 2,000th week at work.

118. Celebrate your 2,000th week of being alive.

119. Celebrate your 2,000th week of exercise.

120. Celebrate your 2,000th week of doing what you said you would do.

121. Repeat this phrase 2000 times: "I am important because I am."

122. Treat yourself to 2000 pleasant memories from your past.

123. Visualize 2000 people celebrating the new M with you.

124. Give away 2000 yo-yos.

125. Give away 2000 hula hoops.

126. Give away 2000 bandannas.

127. Give away 2000 pennies.

128. Take a 2,000-mile train trip.

129. Log 2,000 miles on a plane.

130. Cruise 2,000 miles of ocean.

131. Bike 2,000 miles across the country.

132. Count 2,000 stars.

133. Reward the 2,000th person who shows up any place with a big M prize.

134. Collect 2,000 corks from the new M occasions you celebrate.

135. Buy 2,000 shares of stock.

136. Bunji jump 2,000 feet.

137. Buy an hourglass with 2,000 grains of sand.

138. Practice anything you really want to excel at 2,000 times during the new M.

139. Create a list of 2,000 words of wisdom and carry these with you wherever you go.

140. Climb a 2,000 foot mountain.

141. Give away 2,000 new M car shades.

142. Have a constellation party to identify 2,000 stars.

143. Start a $2,000 M scholarship.

144. Drink 2,000 ounces of water this year.

145. Sponsor a recipe contest for the best 2,000 recipes.

146. Study 2,000 new words in the dictionary.

147. Gather 2,000 names for any petition or drive in the new M.

148. Register 2,000 new voters in your district.

149. Buy 2,000 Krispy Kreme Donuts and share them!

150. Try to meet 2,000 new and interesting people during the new M.

151. Write a M chain letter to 2,000 people.

152. Fly 2,000 miles in a hot air balloon.

153. Collect 2,000 coins and stamps from around the world.

154. Engrave 2,000 beautiful pens with a new M message and pass them out.

155. Start an e-mail "chain letter" of great ways to celebrate the new M and don't stop until you reach 2,000 ideas.

156. Hold hands with 2,000 people in an arena and celebrate being together in the new M.

157. Hold a procession at night with 2,000 people and 2,000 candles to mark the moment.

158. Put up 2,000 banners that celebrate the great moments of the last M in your community.

159. Do 2,000 sit ups during the year.

160. Buy ten $200 bottles of champagne.

161. Reduce the stress in your life by 2,000 minutes.

162. Reduce your debt by $2,000.

163. Reduce your time in front of the TV by 2,000 minutes a month.

164. Read 2,000 words each day (that's about 8 pages).

165. Create a parade with 2,000 entries.

166. Write a book about the top 2,000 people who made a difference in our world during the past M.

167. Record the most memorable event of each day for the first 2,000 days of the new M.

168. Tie a balloon bouquet on every street sign with a 2,000 block number.

169. Eliminate 2,000 grams of fat in your diet this year.

170. Eat 2,000 fresh fruits and vegetables during the first year of the new M.

171. Reduce your caloric intake 2,000 calories per week.

172. Plant 2,000 rose bushes in a cemetery.

173. String together a 2,000 piece popcorn garland for your backyard birds.

174. Spend 2,000 minutes in church.

175. Discard 2000 pounds of unused stuff at your house.

176. Shake 2,000 different hands during the year.

177. Spend 2,000 minutes pampering yourself.

178. Spend at least 2,000 minutes getting to know your neighbors.

179. Believe in yourself for 2,000 seconds (only 34 minutes).

180. Believe in yourself for 2,000 minutes (only 34 hours).

181. Believe in yourself for 2,000 hours (only 34 days).

182. Believe in yourself for 2,000 days (less than 5 1/2 years).

183. Fill a bowl with 2,000 jelly beans.

184. Fill a bowl with 2,000 peanuts.

185. Fill a bowl with 2,000 M&Ms.

186. Fill a bowl with 2,000 peppermints.

187. Fill a bowl with 2,000 chocolate kisses.

188. Fill a bowl with 2,000 Fortune cookies.

189. Give away 2,000 bottles of bubble bath.

190. Give away 2,000 bottles of bubbly.

191. Give away 2,000 bottles of soap bubbles.

192. Collect 2,000 of your favorite bubble gum cards.

193. Put 2,000 pinwheels in an open field.

194. Tie 2,000 balloons in a public place.

195. Put 2,000 pink flamingoes in your yard.

196. Do something memorable on the 2000th hour of the new M.

197. Do something memorable on the 2000th day of the new M.

198. Design a quilt with 2,000 pieces.

199. Have a pajama party with your friends to watch 2,000 minutes of back-to-back, all-time favorite movies.

200. Create 2,000 bags of confetti and pass them out.

201. Collect 2,000 old pennies.

202. Collect 2,000 Millennium pennies.

203. Collect 2,000 things in your favorite color.

204. Walk in 2,000 people's different shoes.

205. Collect 2,000 trading cards of your favorite athletes.

206. Jump rope 2,000 times.

207. Make a wish for 2,000 days at exactly 11:11 for good luck.

208. Come up with 200 different ways to honor the Ten Commandments.

209. Make a "Honey Do" list of 2,000 items. (It will take a Millennium to complete them!)

New Century

[A Note to Our Readers: It may be Year 2000, but it's also a New Century. Here are alternative ways to numerically mark the moment!]

210. Try beers brewed by 100-year-old companies.

211. Visit 100 senior citizens in nursing homes in your area.

212. Put 100 of your favorite photos in your new M album.

213. Rent a bus and take 100 of your best buddies on a road trip.

214. Pass on your 100-years of wisdom and life experiences.

215. Visit an historical site that made a difference in the past 100 years.

216. Improve the Earth in one way in the next 100 years.

217. Make a difference one time as an individual in the next 100 years.

218. Read the epitaphs of those who passed away 100 years ago.

219. Record the stories of a 100-year-old retiree.

220. Draw up a list of your top 100 favorite things to do and do them this year.

221. Save every tree that is 100-years-old in your community.

222. Mark every 100-year-old tree in your community with a new M plaque.

223. Restore every 100-year-old structure in your community.

224. Mark every 100-year-old structure in your community with a new M plaque.

225. Discover and cross every 100-year-old bridge in your region.

226. Visit a city that is 100-years-old.

227. Tour a monument that is 100-years-old.

228. Lose 100 ounces of weight this year (note: only 6 1/4 pounds).

229. Read a book that was written 100 years ago.

230. Write a book about the 100 ideas that made a difference in our world.

231. Pick philosophers from 100 years ago and read their most important works.

232. Pick artists from 100 years ago and view their most important works.

233. Design a new M business card with a special motto for the new century.

234. Get a 100-year-old newspaper or magazine to see what was happening then.

235. Buy a bottle of 100-year-old port.

236. Buy a bottle of champagne for $100.

237. Sponsor a national reunion of everyone who is at least 100-years-old.

238. Create a recipe book with old family favorites from the past 100 years.

239. Read 100 of your favorite books.

240. Make 100 of your favorite recipes.

241. Listen to 100 of your favorite songs.

242. Watch 100 of your favorite movies.

243. Hike 100 of your favorite trails.

244. Bike 100 of your favorite paths.

245. Plant 100 of your favorite flowers.

246. Dance to 100 tunes of your favorite era.

247. Collect 100 of your favorite sayings.

248. Party with 100 friends.

249. Cut 100 calories a day from your diet.

250. Quote 100 of your favorite sayings.

251. Visit the world's top 100 beaches.

252. Visit the world's top 100 resorts.

253. Visit the world's top 100 spas.

254. Visit the world's top 100 museums.

255. Visit the world's top 100 cathedrals.

256. Visit the world's top 100 restaurants.

257. Write to the top 100 companies in the world and relay the importance of making a positive difference in the new M.

258. Write to the top 100 leaders in the world in the new M.

259. Watch the top 100 movies of all time.

260. Listen to the top 100 CDs of all time.

261. Find an open field. Organize an M kite-flying contest with at least 100 entries.

262. Call 100 of your past or present friends to tell them how much they have meant to you.

263. Take a 100-day sabbatical anywhere in the world.

264. Ask your children to record 100 favorite wishes and try to fulfill them as parents.

265. Publicize the 100-year-old things in your community so that all can appreciate their age and relevance in the new M.

266. Give away 100 things from your home to a worthy cause.

267. Hold a costume party that features clothing styles from 100-years-ago.

268. Ask 100 friends what their fondest memories of the last century were, and videotape their answers.

269. Learn to count to 100 in a foreign language.

270. Bake a Millennium birthday cake and decorate it with 100 candles.

271. Package a giant gift box with two items from each of the 50 states and call it your "New Century" goody package.

272. Buy 100 shares of stock.

273. Start a Century garden.

274. Identify 100 ways to improve your life.

275. Pick 10 non-profit organizations and donate 10 hours of community service, totaling 100 hours of your time.

276. Visit 100 libraries in the new M.

277. Attend 100 concerts in the new M.

278. Attend 100 plays in the new M.

279. Go dancing 100 times in the new M.

280. Put together a brochure with all the century bike rides in America and title it: "The New Century Rides."

281. Write 100 politicians and express your views.

282. Encourage 100 people to vote.

283. Honor the senior citizens in your community who have passed the 100-year mark.

284. Start believing in yourself. It's a new century.

Fractionals

3

[A Note to Our Readers: Even the smallest steps can lead to success and fulfillment in the new Millennium. Start now!]

285. Run 5.5 miles a day for 365 days.

286. Swim 5.5 laps a day for 365 days.

287. Walk 5.5 miles a day for 365 days.

288. Dance with your loved one for 5.5 minutes a day all year.

289. Take 5.5 minutes a day all year to talk with your loved one.

290. Spend 5.5 minutes a day all year playing with your kids.

291. Encourage your local media to take 5.5 minutes a day all year to promote some "good news."

292. Say "good morning" to 5.5 people a day. (Note: The "half" should be a kid).

293. Listen to your favorite tunes at least 5.5 minutes a day for the year.

294. Pray at least 5.5 minutes a day for the year.

295. Pay at least 5.5 compliments to people a day.

296. Brainstorm 5.5 ideas a day to better your life.

297. Wake up and smell the coffee.

298. Build a sandcastle.

299. Give someone a rose.

300. Sleep in a breeze.

301. Sleep under the stars.

302. Take your kids to the park.

303. Spend a day at the movies.

304. Eat a snow cone.

305. Try taffy candy.

306. Boycott frivolous shopping.

307. Bike to work one day.

308. Wear a carnation in your lapel.

309. Have a yard sale.

310. Go through one day without cursing.

311. Eliminate road rage.

312. Call an old friend.

313. Talk to someone in line.

314. Speak to your neighbors.

315. Help raise money for a good cause.

316. Lend your talent towards a good cause.

317. Put a chocolate on a pillow.

318. Make your bed.

319. If you take it out, put it back.

320. If you make a mess, clean it up.

321. Wax your pickup.

322. Don't yell at your kids.

323. Don't park your truck in your front yard.

324. Eat a jelly donut.

325. Adopt a stray pet.

326. Floss.

327. Slow down.

328. Send a bouquet of flowers to a friend.

329. Help a senior citizen run an errand.

330. Try to be silent one day each month.

331. Listen and learn from what you've experienced.

332. Take one day off for yourself each month.

333. Send a hand-made card to a friend.

334. Lend a helping hand at least once each year.

335. Tip more than generously.

336. Follow a butterfly.

337. Listen to a bird sing.

338. Wear a ballcap.

339. Arrive in a limo.

340. Put your feet up on the coffee table.

341. Play horseshoes.

342. Buy furniture that people enjoy.

343. Make your home comfortable.

344. Stress less.

345. Laugh.

346. Celebrate with crystal.

347. Celebrate with diamonds.

348. Celebrate with sparklers.

349. Celebrate with sparkling cider.

350. Celebrate with sparkling water.

351. Celebrate with anything that sparkles.

352. Wear clothes that express you.

353. Put fountains in your home.

354. Buy an aquarium.

355. Create a water garden in your backyard.

356. Invest in a spa.

357. Build a treehouse for your kids.

358. Ride a rollercoaster.

359. Ride a merry-go-round.

360. Eat healthy.

361. Don't supersize. Downsize.

362. Practice the Golden Rule.

363. Keep your new M resolutions.

364. Go out on a limb.

365. Dare to be unique.

366. Create harmony.

367. Carry a compass.

368. Whistle.

369. Watch a baby being born.

370. Sing in the shower.

371. Go to a drive-in movie.

372. Finish what you start.

373. Lighten up.

374. Let nature be your symphony.

375. Think for yourself.

376. Hold hands more often.

377. Keep your alley clean.

378. Beautify a part of your yard just for you.

379. Embrace life.

380. Smile more often.

381. Hold harmless.

382. Be open-minded.

383. Surprise someone.

384. Say "thank you" more often.

385. Eliminate waste.

386. Enlighten your mind.

387. Try something new.

388. Be more patient.

389. Catch a ride with a friend.

390. Have a cup of coffee with a friend.

391. Call your mom.

392. Carpool at least once.

393. Start a family with love.

394. Bring up a family with love.

395. Say "I love you" more often.

396. Take a bubblebath.

397. Dine in candlelight.

398. Have a mimosa.

399. Use your turn signals.

400. Do something silly.

401. Get married.

402. Find the best burger in town and savor every bite.

403. Find the best pub in town and savor every flavor.

404. Relax in a cozy corner of your favorite bookstore.

405. Fill your senses at a flower shop.

406. Find the music that taps into your soul and listen to it.

407. Walk under the first full moon of the new M.

408. Dance under the first full moon.

409. Follow a rainbow from end to end.

410. Follow a road that you don't know.

411. Take a pleasant detour through the countryside.

412. Stay at a bed and breakfast—and stay late.

413. Have a picnic in the country.

414. Host a family reunion.

415. Embrace the M. Don't fear it.

416. Worry less.

417. Learn to swim.

418. Roast chestnuts over an open fire.

419. Stay out late at least once.

420. Rotate your tires every 7,000 miles.

421. Plan to travel 2,000 miles out of your comfort zone.

422. Give someone a present.

423. Visit an aviary.

424. Visit a butterfly garden.

425. Push with kindness.

426. Nurture your talents.

427. Nurture others' talents.

428. Be truthful.

429. Be faithful.

430. Make it yourself.

431. Help someone grow.

432. Make it count.

433. Go back to school.

434. Follow your heart.

435. Take care of your health.

436. Be yourself.

437. Be proud of your abilities.

438. Develop character.

439. Get back to the basics.

440. Seek happiness within yourself.

441. Lean on someone.

442. Ask for help.

443. Grow old together.

444. You're as young as you feel.

445. Get involved.

446. Be genuine.

447. Stay focused.

448. Be positive.

449. Learn to be a good parent.

450. Practice being a patient parent.

451. Embrace imperfections.

452. Try at least twice.

453. Learn from your mistakes.

454. Value your time.

455. Save first. Spend later.

456. Make a paper airplane.

457. Experience all the four seasons.

458. Walk barefoot in the grass.

459. Make a whistle out of a blade of grass.

460. Find a four-leaf clover.

461. Make sun tea.

462. Respect all of God's creatures.

463. Place some windchimes in a breezy path.

464. Embrace challenges.

465. Create opportunities.

466. Design a backyard oasis.

467. Care for the things you have.

468. Remember who has helped you.

469. Don't keep up with the Joneses.

470. Remember your beginnings.

471. Don't put pressure on yourself all the time.

472. Try not to stub your toe.

473. Make homemade biscuits.

474. Find beauty wherever you look.

475. Share a shower.

476. Give yourself permission.

477. Send a card when it's not a holiday.

478. Take time to care.

479. Let yourself to cry.

480. Deal with reality.

481. Learn to say, "I'm sorry."

482. Be the first to say, "I'm sorry."

483. Learn to laugh at yourself.

484. Buy a good shower head.

485. Don't knock it until you've tried it.

486. Rock the boat.

487. Make life grand.

488. Share a good bottle of wine with friends.

489. Cut your roses and fill your vases.

490. Pick up the pieces.

491. Have a piece of chocolate fudge cake!

492. Don't live in denial.

493. It's your life. Take charge.

494. Sleep in a good bed.

495. Beach it.

496. If you can't think of something good to say, keep thinking.

497. Write an M recipe.

498. Write an M joke.

499. Celebrate our differences.

500. Make one dream come true.

501. Enter a tournament with your kid.

502. Be in a parade!

503. Share a good conversation with a friend.

504. Don't make commitments you can't keep.

505. Watch your words!

506. Use a good bar of soap.

507. Forgive yourself.

508. Treat yourself.

509. Believe in yourself.

510. Be yourself.

511. Venture outside your routine boundaries.

512. Eliminate your credit card debt this year.

513. Reduce your credit cards by one.

514. Pamper yourself.

515. Before you decide, look at both sides.

516. Avoid worrying about what hasn't happened.

517. Don't be a time watcher.

518. Don't be a time waster.

519. Increase your brainpower.

520. Read more often.

521. Let your children make mistakes.

522. Find a way to make it happen.

523. Enjoy moments of silence.

524. If you think life is all about money, think again.

525. You don't have to look far to find the good in life.

526. Count your blessings, not your bank account.

527. Today is a good time to start believing in yourself.

528. Put a new greeting on your phone every day during the new M.

529. Eat a peanut butter and jelly sandwich.

530. Fix your favorite childhood dinner.

531. Fix your favorite snack as a kid.

532. Frame your favorite family photo.

533. Be flexible when someone asks you for a favor.

534. Read a book someone else recommends to you.

535. Go see a foreign film like "Life is Beautiful."

536. Go to the IMAX theater.

537. Go to the $1 movies.

538. Try a new wine once a month and learn something about its origins.

539. Listen to a new musician once a month and get to know his or her musical background.

540. Visit an art gallery once a month and learn about the different styles of painting.

541. Go to the theater once a month and enjoy a play you've never seen.

542. Get tickets to a different sporting event each month and learn something about that sport.

543. Take a different bike path.

544. Take a different route to work.

545. Throw an M picnic in the park and invite your friends.

546. Try shuffleboard.

547. Shoot darts.

548. Play pool.

549. Learn chicken foot.

550. Buy your favorite childhood game and play it.

551. Camp in a tent.

552. Learn to play bridge.

553. Ride a horse.

554. Take your child fishing.

555. Save a tadpole.

556. Drive out to the country for a catfish dinner.

557. Learn the art of knot tying.

558. Learn how to use a yo-yo.

559. Learn how to spin a top.

560. Learn how to play jacks.

561. Learn how to play hop scotch.

562. Learn how to jump rope.

563. Donate your used books to a local library.

564. Clean out your attic.

565. Clean out your cellar.

566. Fix something that's broken.

567. If it's not broken, don't fix it.

568. Place some chimes where the wind blows.

569. Change your life.

570. Frame your silliest photo.

571. Rain or shine, get out more often.

572. Plant honeysuckle on your fence.

573. Visit an aquarium.

574. Put an aquarium in your home.

575. Just relax.

576. Give yourself a break.

577. Improve a little corner of your lot.

578. Keep a new M resolution.

579. Write a toast to your mom.

580. Share your favorite music with a member of another generation.

581. Show you care every day.

582. Learn to politely say "no."

583. Learn to say "yes" when it's not always on your terms.

584. Take one skill and hone it.

585. Try something new.

586. Try something again, even if you've failed at it.

587. Sit on a park bench and people watch.

588. Ask someone to dance.

589. Go on a blind date.

590. Pray for peace.

591. Dedicate a poem to a friend.

592. Once a month, pick a town called "Fate," or "Hope," or something inspiring, and go visit the town.

593. Find a pen pal.

594. Collect a postcard from every major city in the world.

595. Commit yourself to one community project.

596. Get a new bathing suit.

597. Buy some sexy pajamas.

598. Make a campfire.

599. Throw skipping stones across a pond.

600. Go skinny dipping.

601. Create a tranquillity spot in your garden.

602. Nap in a hammock.

603. For every problem, find two solutions.

604. Watch a baby bird fly for the first time.

605. Believe you can do it!

606. Update your resume.

607. Devote yourself to your family.

608. Pray every day.

609. Create a special book of "work and love" coupons for your family to redeem in the new M.

610. Write an M cookbook with generations of your family's recipes.

611. Make new M keepsake albums for your grandchildren.

612. Start a newborn album for every child who enters the new M.

613. Bronze your baby's shoes for the new M.

614. Take a plaster impression of your new baby's hands or feet to remember them in the new Millennium.

615. Spend an evening with your family remembering 2,000 things that you have shared together.

616. If you can't think of 2,000, make it 100 to mark the moment.

617. Eliminate one act of violence that your child may view everyday.

618. Write a book with your family of its history.

619. Make a really fine meal for you to share with your family or friends.

620. Sit down together with your family at dinner and take the time to really talk to each other.

621. Create a postcard of you and your family celebrating the new M.

622. Create a photo collage of family members past and present.

623. Write a special note of 2,000 words to your mom.

624. Tell your loved ones you love them—2,000 times.

625. Spend 2,000 extra minutes a month with your kids.

626. Write 2,000 ideas for your kids about how to succeed in life.

627. Celebrate your 2,000th week of being a family.

628. Create a video that reflects on 2,000 of your family's most important memories.

629. Take 2,000 minutes of your time to talk with your kids.

630. Take your family on a hay ride.

631. Take your family on a sleigh ride.

632. Take your family on a horse and buggy ride.

633. Put together a 2,000 picture collage of your family and your life.

634. Go bowling with your buddies, and reward the first bowler who reaches 2,000 points.

635. Tell your spouse you love him or her on the 2,000th second of the new M.

636. Tell your spouse you love him or her 2,000 times.

637. Play a game with friends and the first one to score 2,000 points wins.

638. Spend at least 2,000 seconds (less than 34 minutes!) with your dad on Father's Day.

639. Spend at least 2,000 seconds with your grandmother or grandfather on their birthdays.

640. Spend at least 2,000 seconds with your brothers or sisters on their birthdays.

641. Read your favorite childhood books to your children.

642. Swap houses with another family in another part of the country or the world to celebrate the new M.

643. Don't know a family to swap with? Log onto www.intervac.org You'll be able to list your home and have access to thousands of fellow M house swappers for a small fee.

644. Do a dine around at your favorite restaurants.

645. Do a dine around at the homes of your friends.

646. Give a foot rub to your loved one at least once a week.

647. Give a head rub to your loved one at least once a week.

648. Give a back rub to your loved one at least once a week.

649. Brainstorm with your friends about what you can do to ensure the next M.

650. Take a trip with your best friends.

651. Record the stories of your grandparents.

652. Record the stories of your parents.

653. Record the stories of you and your family.

654. Create a coupon book of new M promises and give it to a special friend to redeem.

655. Start a hope chest for your children for the new M.

656. Have a family reunion.

657. Do an extra chore for your parents every day.

658. Adopt a child who needs your love.

659. Spend 2,000 minutes on home improvement projects.

660. Make one major home improvement.

661. Try to find a friend with whom you've lost touch.

662. Rent a local movie theater and invite your friends for a midnight movie party.

663. Book an entire hotel or bed and breakfast for you, your family and friends.

664. Pour a small section of concrete near your home and imprint your hands and the date to remember the new M.

665. Arrange a reunion of your family.

666. Arrange a reunion with your best friends.

667. Treat your family to a Saturday afternoon at the movies.

668. Keep a new M scrapbook to hand down to future generations.

669. Go see the AIDS Quilt. It is woven with love and compassion and serves as a constant reminder of the cures yet to be found.

670. Visit one of the haunted places described in the book, *Haunted Places: The National Directory.* Maybe, you'll meet the ghost of the new M!

671. Engrave a silver spoon with your name and the Year 2000 and pass it down as an heirloom.

672. Get together with your family or best friends at a lodge, campgrounds, or private cabin to celebrate.

673. Just give in to your kids and party at home. Your pets might panic, but bring them treats, too, and you'll all be dancing and blowing horns at midnight!

674. Charter a bus with your best friends and drive to the "Price is Right Show."

675. Fill a cooler with beer and listen to tunes with friends that carry you back several decades.

676. Fill a cooler with champagne and listen to tunes with friends that carry you back several decades.

677. Fill a bucket with champagne and dance under the stars with your friends.

678. Fill a cooler with beer and champagne and reminisce about the beer and champagne moments in your life with your best friends.

679. Set up an outdoor bonfire with your neighbors and reminisce together.

680. Go to family night at your local bowling alley.

681. Take a photo at midnight 2000 of you and your family.

682. Take a photo of you at midnight 2000.

683. Take a photo of you and your best friends at midnight 2000.

684. Party at the First Night International event to be staged in 200 large and small cities. It's a non-alcoholic evening so you can bring the kids, too. To find the one nearest you, log onto www.firstnightintl.org

685. Create a wish list for your partner in life and try to fulfill each other's wishes.

686. Create a wish list for family members and try to fulfill each other's wishes.

687. Create a wish list for friends and try to fulfill each other's wishes.

688. Create a family tree for the new M.

689. Visit a distant relative in the new M.

690. Visit the sites where your relatives have been buried.

691. Look at all your photo albums of past years.

692. Look at all your family videos of past years.

693. Treat your partner to a day of beauty.

694. Treat your best friend to a day of beauty.

695. Treat your mom to a day of beauty.

696. Treat your dad to a round of golf.

697. Go to the zoo for the day with your family.

698. Go to a theme park for the day with your friends.

699. Brainstorm ways you and your family can share the M together.

700. Celebrate another culture on New Year's Day.

701. Celebrate anything more often with your family.

702. Adopt a senior citizen at a nursing home.

703. Build something with your hands for your home.

704. Try doing it yourself.

705. Ask your family what they would like to do on the first day of the M.

706. Treat yourself to a baby-sitter and do something as a couple.

707. Arrange a bus trip with your best friends to celebrate.

708. Take a group picture with friends and family. If you're not all in the same town, find a central gathering place.

709. Frame your favorite photo of your friends.

710. Frame your favorite photo of you and your dad.

711. Frame your favorite photo of you and your mom.

712. Frame your favorite photo of you and your kids.

713. Frame your favorite photo of you and your spouse.

714. Frame your favorite photo of you and your boyfriend or girlfriend.

715. Create a family crest for the new M.

716. Ask your pastor to bestow an M blessing on your family.

717. Visit the city, state, or country where your family originated.

718. Brainstorm ways to bring new meaning into your family's life for the new M.

719. Call everyone who's made a difference in your life on the first day of the M.

720. Remember those who are no longer here to celebrate the M.

721. Put fresh flowers on a loved one's grave.

722. Renew your wedding vows.

723. Renew them under a full moon.

724. Renew them at a sunrise service.

725. Renew them in the springtime.

726. Renew them in a winter wonderland.

727. Renew them throughout the seasons of your life.

Pets

6

[A Note to Our Readers: Okay, so this is a short section about a very popular topic—your pets. We just didn't want you to forget these great and loyal creatures as they run, jump, climb, hop, fly, swim, and walk into the new M with you!]

728. Name a pet for the new M.

729. Spring for special new M pet tags.

730. Buy your dog a 2,000 M sweater.

731. Buy yourself a matching 2,000 M sweater.

732. Have your kids donate 2,000 pennies to the SPCA.

733. Make a commitment to walk your dog everyday.

734. If you're ready for the responsibility, adopt a puppy or kitty from the SPCA.

735. Take a portrait of your pets.

736. Get your community to adopt or spay and neuter 2,000 pets.

737. Create new M hairstyles for your pets.

738. Treat your pets to a Millennium Bash at one of the Best Friends Pet Resorts. There are 35 of them in the U.S. Plans call for a howl-off contest and lots of canine and feline party treats. For more info, call toll-free 1-888-FOR-PETS.

739. Hug 2,000 pets (unless you have allergies!).

740. Take a photo of you and your favorite pet at midnight 2000.

741. Frame your favorite photo of you and your pet.

742. Give a stuffed pet to every kid at a local hospital or orphanage.

743. Create an M collage of all your pets.

744. Pet your pets 2,000 times this year.

745. Treat your pets to a day of beauty.

746. Walk your dog at least 2,000 feet each week.

747. Play with your pets at least 2,000 minutes in the new M.

Seasonal

7

[Note to Our Readers: Yes, we admit, this section is sparse, too. But we're confident you can think of some superb seasonal opportunities to mark the moment!]

748. Host an Easter egg hunt with 2,000 eggs.

749. Pass out 2,000 miniature flags on the fourth of July.

750. Roast 2,000 hot dogs on the fourth of July.

751. Light 2,000 sparklers to celebrate.

752. Give away 2,000 pounds of turkey on Thanksgiving Day.

753. Send out 2,000 Valentine's cards.

754. Give away 2,000 lucky pennies on St. Patrick's Day.

755. Pass out 2,000 party horns on New Year's Day!

756. Share a round of 2,000 ounces of green beer on St. Patrick's Day with everyone in the bar.

757. Plant a living Christmas tree in your neighborhood park and put a marker on it for the new M.

758. Coordinate a horn blowing with your entire community on January 1, 2000.

759. Ring your church bells on January 1, 2000.

760. Start a Civic 2000 group which explores ways to make improvements throughout the M.

761. Form a Teens 2000 group to represent the voice of youth in your community during the new M.

762. Volunteer 2,000 minutes of your time to a worthy cause.

763. Introduce yourself to new neighbors.

764. Tear down your privacy fence.

765. Don't let your homeowners association control your life.

766. Cook 2,000 black-eyed peas and share them with your neighbors.

767. Write a check for $2,000 to your favorite charity.

768. Donate 2,000 lucky pennies ($20) to your favorite charity.

769. Donate 2,000 immunization shots to the needy.

770. Donate 2,000 ice cream cups to children's charities.

771. Give away 2,000 baby diapers to new moms in the new M.

772. Vaccinate 2,000 kids and elderly.

773. Visit 2,000 people in retirement homes.

774. Collect 2,000 coats or sweaters and give them to charity.

775. Have a car wash for 2,000 cars and donate the money to charity.

776. Spend 2,000 minutes as a Big Brother or Sister.

777. Hold a community garage sale featuring 2,000 items.

778. Reduce the number of crime victims by 2,000 in your state.

779. Reduce the number of teenage pregnancies by 2,000.

780. Reduce the number of lawsuits in your state by 2,000.

781. Come up with 2,000 solutions to better your community.

782. Create a video about 2,000 of the most important milestones in your community's history.

783. Form a neighborhood "Walk & Watch" program for a safer community. Ask each walker to donate 2,000 minutes towards its success.

784. Sell 2,000 bricks to be inscribed for the new M. Then, donate them for a walkway in a local park.

785. Create a video about 2,000 of the most important people from your community.

786. Get 2,000 people off welfare and into new jobs this new M.

787. Make 2,000 improvements in your community no matter how small.

788. Make 2,000 improvements in your state no matter how small.

789. Donate 2,000 points from your frequent anything program to a worthy cause.

790. Help Habitat for Humanity build 2,000 new homes.

791. Solicit 2,000 people to donate a book to your local library or recreation center.

792. Take a group photo with 2,000 people in it.

793. Give 2,000 bags of food to the needy.

794. Donate 2,000 bags of clothing for the needy.

795. Find one way to improve your community in the next century.

796. Find one way to improve your country in the next century.

797. Give away 2,000 Beanie babies to a children's charity.

798. Engrave 2,000 names of senior citizens who have made the greatest lifetime contributions to your community and put a plaque on a facility to honor them.

799. Collect 2,000 pairs of shoes for the needy.

800. Collect 2,000 eyeglasses for the needy.

801. Collect 2,000 coats for the needy.

802. Hire a group of clowns to visit 2,000 sick kids and elderly.

803. Arrange for an M retrospective in the arts, music, dance, and letters to celebrate.

804. Invite artists, sculptors, musicians, and other craftspeople to define the new M through a special exhibit for the public.

805. Visit 2,000 different schools and choose one to help.

806. Pick one public wall and inscribe it with advice for kids entering the new M.

807. Showcase the last three Millennia with artifacts, mementos, and memorabilia.

808. Host a series of M events throughout your community like bike rallies, walks, runs, concerts, and other outdoor events.

809. Establish an outstanding M service award.

810. Host a seminar of great M futurists.

811. Host a seminar of new M authors.

812. Create an M Kindness Bank to match needy organizations with the in-kind contributions of local businesses.

813. Participate in the Millennium photo project. Check it out at www.millenniumphoto.com

814. Publish a guide that lists 2,000 reasons why your community is great.

815. Adopt a community project to help your senior citizens.

816. Adopt a community project to help your local schools.

817. Adopt a community project to help your local businesses.

818. Adopt a community project to help your local SPCA.

819. If you're a rural community, join neighboring communities and create an M project together.

820. If you're in a rural community, sponsor a Millennium walk from town to town. Make it a candlelight walk or moonlight walk for all to enjoy.

821. Design an M sculpture for your community.

822. Give your town a new M facelift.

823. Start a public servant of the year award in the new M.

824. Participate in a community activity once a month.

825. Broadcast favorite TV shows of each decade during the M.

826. Create an art exhibit of the greatest artists of the past M.

827. Create an exhibit of the greatest people and influences of the past M.

828. Name a street in your town in honor of the new M.

829. Thank every volunteer.

830. Save your community's historical landmarks.

831. Sponsor a new M bazaar with 2,000 merchants from your community.

832. Place inspirational mottoes for the new M in a public garden.

833. Light 2,000 candles in the memory of those who have served your community and are no longer here to celebrate the new M.

834. Install a commemorative bench in honor of the new M in any public place.

835. Gather ministers of all faiths and host a 24-hour worship service in a public park.

836. Stage a series of M concerts in your community. Feature new bands.

837. Stage a series of M art shows in your community. Feature new artists.

838. Invite 2,000 choir members to sing together to celebrate the new M.

839. Sponsor an M ice sculpting contest.

840. Sponsor an M dance contest.

841. Sponsor an M photography contest.

842. Sponsor an M art contest.

843. Sponsor an M car rally.

844. Sponsor an M slam poetry session.

845. Sponsor an M open mike session.

846. Send flowers to everyone in a local nursing home.

847. Send new M greetings to everyone in a local nursing home.

848. Send flowers to everyone in a nearby hospital.

849. Send new M greetings to everyone in a nearby hospital.

850. Have your arboretum design a 2,000 flower-shaped new M display.

851. Have the city give the 2,000th person who pays taxes a $200 break.

852. Have the city give the 2,000th person who pays the water bill a free month off.

853. Have the library give the 2,000th visitor a new M history book.

854. Hold a community hero of the new M contest.

855. Honor the top community volunteer of the new M.

856. Put up "Welcome to the New M, [your community's name here]" banners.

857. Ask everyone in your community to donate just $1 for a special M project to beautify your community.

858. Engrave the names of every citizen in your community on a plaque and install it in a public place to mark the moment.

859. Sponsor a community costume contest to create the best costume from the last M.

860. Hold a 2,000 canned goods drive for your community food bank.

861. Have a new M community fair with a $2,000 prize or new car raffle.

862. Hold a 2,000 person parade down main street.

863. Ask your school district to honor the 2,000 top students in your community.

864. Honor the Year 2000 mom who has overcome great obstacles.

865. Offer discounted pet services to 2,000 animals, based on the owner's financial needs.

866. Hang new M flags over your main street.

867. Create an M reading section at your library.

868. Fund an M mural for public view.

869. Dedicate an event, street, or public space after an individual who has made the greatest difference in your community during the past M.

870. Elect a Citizen for the Day on the first day of the new M.

871. Create commemorative new M t-shirts for your entire community.

872. Name a building for the new M.

873. If you're good at a craft, teach someone who wants to learn it.

874. If you have a special talent, share it with others in your community.

875. Tap into the lost crafts of senior citizens. Invite them to teach your group how to whittle, fiddle, quilt or weave.

876. Create a community "how to" book of these lost arts from breadmaking to needlepoint.

877. Adopt a senior citizen and spend a week learning from him or her.

878. Adopt a school and spend a week there. Brainstorm ideas to help the school.

879. Adopt a non-profit and spend a week learning how to help it.

880. Make 2,000 improvements in your region no matter how small.

881. Declare an M Family Night Out.

882. Turn on the lights throughout your community on the first night of the new M.

883. Take 2,000 gallons of paint and spruce up your community.

School

[A Note to Our Readers: What better way to celebrate than to do something for education? Or something for yourself? Or just something that brings the old high school and college crowd back together to remember the good times?]

884. Reduce the number of dropouts by 2,000 in your state.

885. Adopt a team and spend a week cheering for them.

886. Sponsor a team, too.

887. If you're a new school opening in the M, pick a song, mascot and uniform that ties into it.

888. Increase the IQ of your student body by 2,000.

889. Make your school yearbook a special M edition.

890. Create a special M edition of your school paper.

891. Give away $2,000 in computer hardware or software to your local school.

892. Have an M reunion of teachers and students.

893. Have a new M reunion for all the students who became politicians in your high school or college.

894. Have a new M reunion for all the students who became educators in your high school or college.

895. Have a new M reunion for all the students who became entrepreneurs in your high school or college.

896. Host a multi-disciplinary job fair with former graduates from your high school or college.

897. Create an M commemorative t-shirt from your school or college.

898. Throw a high school M graduation party. Invite every class back to celebrate!

899. Throw a college M graduation party. Invite every class back celebrate!

900. Rent your dream car to go to your high school or college reunion.

901. Learn a new language during the M.

902. Establish an M scholarship for a deserving student.

903. Theme your spring break around the M.

904. Create a special M rush week.

905. Salute the best teachers of the past M in your community with a pictorial profile in your local paper.

906. Get a new degree during the M.

907. Release 2,000 balloons at any graduation.

908. Engrave 2,000 names of the best students in your high school or college and place a plaque on your building to honor them.

909. Have a reunion of any high school or college class with 2,000 seniors.

910. Donate 2,000 books to your neighborhood library or school.

911. Rent the school auditorium and host a Year 2000 reunion in it.

912. Create a video about the 2,000 most important milestones in your high school's history.

913. Create a video about the 2,000 most important milestones in your college's history.

914. Create an M patch for your school activity uniforms.

915. Sponsor a debate about the M's impact.

916. Visit your old high school during the M.

917. Visit your favorite teacher.

918. Get together with your class and donate something special to your high school or college for the new M.

919. For proms and homecomings, theme your event and door prizes for the M.

920. Engrave your high school or college ring with an M quote.

921. Sponsor an M lecture series.

922. Attend a high school sporting event.

923. Attend a college sporting event.

924. Theme the first week back to school for the new M.

925. Hold a schoolwide contest for the best ideas for the new M to improve your school.

926. Endow an M chair in research at your local college or university.

927. Create an M education fund.

928. Hold a school pep rally to celebrate the new M.

929. Form an M pen pal group with a class from across the globe.

930. Do your part to eliminate teen violence for the new M.

931. Circulate a petition for your school stating, "I will not succumb to peer pressure."

932. Offer $2,000 scholarships to the top graduating high school senior for every high school in your community.

933. Write a new M positive rap song. There is good in everyone's life.

934. If you're an auto maker, create a Millennium hood ornament.

935. If you're a teacher, assign your students a new M documentary project.

936. If you're a cyber junkie, create your own M web site or zine.

937. If you're a chef, create a special M menu.

938. If you're an artist, render the new M through your eyes.

939. If you're a trainer, suggest techniques for succeeding in the new M.

940. If you're a futurist, project your ideas for the new M.

941. If you're an entrepreneur, design a new M gadget.

942. If you're an author, create a new M race that dazzles our imagination.

943. If you're a celebrity, do something great that others can imitate for the new M.

944. If you're an architect, suggest new models for homes and offices in the new M.

945. If you're a software designer, develop a program that capitalizes on the best of the new M.

946. If you're a scientist, discover cures to our worst illnesses.

947. If you're a computer geek, find 2,000 ways to get a "people life."

948. If you're an umpire, create an M flipping coin.

949. If you're a rock collector, collect 2,000 rocks.

950. If you're a retail salesperson, call your first 2,000 customers by name.

951. If you're a nurse, pass out 2,000 "Health Is Power" buttons for patients to wear.

952. If you're parents, save $2,000 a year for college for your kids.

953. If you're a car collector, hold an M car exhibit with classics from the past and prototypes for the future.

954. If you're a government worker, take 20 minutes to list 100 ways the government can save money.

955. If you're a journalist, research and create an M year wrap-up.

956. If you're a bartender, create your signature M drink.

957. If you're a photographer, compile an M photo journal.

958. If you're a pizza delivery person, write Happy 2000 on the top of each pizza box.

959. If you're a CEO, ask your employees for 2,000 ways to improve your company.

960. If you're a secretary, make sure your CEO reads these ideas and acts upon them.

961. If you're a salesperson, create a list of 2,000 ways to serve your clients better, improve your prospecting techniques, and increase your income.

962. If you're a computer expert, help your friends avoid a Y2K crash.

963. If you're a bottler, print M messages on your bottle caps or labels.

964. If you're a photography teacher, assign your students an M photo contest.

965. If you're an architect, sponsor an exhibit of building designs from the past and prototypes for the future.

966. If you're a doctor, create an exhibit of medical breakthroughs of the past and concepts for the future.

967. If you're a farmer, create an exhibit of old tools from the past and new tools for the present.

968. For teachers, bring in something from the past, the present, and ideas for the future.

969. For boat lovers, have a boat parade for the M.

970. For ministers of faith, theme your sermons around a special M message.

971. For teachers, discuss the meaning and history of the word "M."

972. For artists, interpret the M through your artwork.

973. For retailers, stockpile your best Y2K goods and create displays that promote them.

974. For entrepreneurs, capitalize on the Y2K crisis. Make it fun. Make it helpful.

975. If you love golf, play the course of your dreams.

976. If you love tennis, play the court of your dreams.

977. If you love baseball, play the field of your dreams.

978. If you love skiing, ski the slopes of your dreams.

979. If you love sunbathing, bask by the sea of your dreams.

980. If you love hiking, follow the trail of your dreams.

981. If you love climbing, ascend the mountain of your dreams.

982. If you love sailing, skim the lake of your dreams.

983. If you love racing, drive the course of your dreams.

Positive Things

11

[Note to Our Readers: Let's face it, there are many things that happen that are out of our control. It's up to you to initiate the positive things in your life. Make these happen in the new M for you!]

984. Create a dream board for your life. Begin with the first day of the new M.

985. Learn your family history.

986. Get rid of annoying alarm clocks.

987. Wake up to music everyday.

988. Simplify your life.

989. Get rid of something every week that you rarely use.

990. Create your own horoscope each day.

991. Do something that's healthy for you every day.

992. Treat yourself to a day of beauty.

993. Eliminate one bad thought a day for the new M.

994. Smoke one less cigarette a day for the new M.

995. Make a wish every day.

996. Accomplish one goal every day for the new M, no matter how small.

997. Celebrate living long enough to enter the new M.

998. Read a positive story in the newspaper everyday.

999. Buy a painting that inspires you.

1000. Buy a photograph that inspires you.

1001. Skip work one day and celebrate being alive.

1002. Take a nap in front of a woodburning fireplace.

1003. Be spontaneous.

1004. Enjoy every adventure in the new M.

1005. Dedicate a poem to the new M.

1006. Collect a coin from every year during the last M.

1007. Order a special M edition of anything.

1008. Take a family portrait to commemorate the M.

1009. Have an M baby shower.

1010. Record what you were doing at the turn of the new M.

1011. Invest in a telescope and see the stars.

1012. Get a special license plate to mark the moment.

1013. Start a coin collection of new M coins.

1014. Make a new M quilt.

1015. Start a stamp collection of new M stamps.

1016. Upgrade all your old gadgets with new M gadgets.

1017. Treat yourself to a new restaurant once a month for a year.

1018. Stock up on champagne. The prices will triple by New Year's Eve!

1019. Start the M by paying yourself first. This is the only way to build your nest egg.

1020. Take to heart, "You only live once!" And live it in Year 2000.

1021. Grow old gracefully but stay young at heart!

1022. Start using your china and silver for everyday occasions.

1023. If you own neither china nor silver, buy your first setting to celebrate.

1024. If you cannot afford a setting, go antique shopping. You'll discover many "finds".

1025. Send "Happy New M" e-mails wishing people health, happiness and prosperity.

1026. Make a quilt with bits of clothing from every decade.

1027. Postmark an envelope to commemorate the new M.

1028. Participate in at least one M event.

1029. Be happy every day this new M.

1030. Make a needlepoint design that marks the moment!

1031. Send a "heartfelt" pizza to someone you love in the new M. Place the pepperoni on the pizza in the shape of a heart.

1032. Hand out a "Happy M" business card.

1033. Save your wine corks and date them with your M moments.

1034. Write an M prescription for happiness and carry it in your pocket.

1035. Compile a special M photo album.

1036. Pick your favorite parades in all your favorite cities and go watch them!

1037. Write your predictions for the new M and see how many come true by year-end.

1038. Drop the word "never" from your vocabulary.

1039. Learn to play the instrument you always wanted to as a child.

1040. Collect something memorable from each decade you've been alive.

1041. Learn a new sport during the M.

1042. Exercise your right to vote during the new M.

1043. Do something this year because you want to, not because you have to.

1044. Watch a movie from every decade.

1045. Subscribe to the History Channel and learn from the past M.

1046. Do something that makes you feel good every day, as long as it's healthy for you.

1047. Make one improvement in your life.

1048. Send out a new M greeting card with confetti in it.

1049. Send an electronic M greeting over the Internet.

1050. Send a new M box with a party hat and blower in it.

1051. Gather all your favorite sayings, cartoons, and fortune cookie notes and organize your top 2,000 into a new M book.

1052. Wake up with cheer in your voice and your heart.

1053. Make a list of 2,000 positive words to have in your vocabulary.

1054. Make a new M list of positive things you've always wanted to do and do them.

1055. Record the obstacles you encounter during the new M, and, later, review the good that came from them.

1056. Keep a new M positive diary and list all the positive experi-

1057. Make a list of your favorite positive Bible quotes and read them every day.

1058. Send your list of positive statements to a friend.

1059. Start a Year 2000 list called "Why I Love Myself," and add one reason every day.

1060. Take a trip to a foreign country this year.

1061. See one of the wonders of the world.

1062. If time and money permit, see all the wonders of the world.

1063. Send a greeting card to loved ones for every occasion during the new M.

1064. Keep a notebook of each marked moment.

1065. Mark the new M every day with a favor, a kind word, and a gift of love.

1066. Forgive everyone you haven't forgiven in the new M.

1067. Adopt a charity for the M.

1068. Adopt a kid for the M.

1069. Adopt a pet for the M.

1070. Adopt a senior citizen for the M.

1071. If you're not happy with your life up to this moment, change it. It's a new M.

1072. Eliminate one bad habit for the new M.

1073. Dare to do something you've always avoided.

1074. Dare to do something you've always longed to do.

1075. Dare to do something you never thought you could do.

1076. Dare to do something you believed you could do but haven't.

1077. Keep a Year 2000 memoir of what you've learned from each day of the new M.

1078. Put your favorite affirmation or saying on a new M coffee mug.

1079. Put your favorite affirmation or saying on a new M t-shirt.

1080. Say "I love myself" 2,000 times.

1081. Say "I forgive you" any amount of times.

1082. Say "I will love you no matter what."

1083. Say "I have the power to reach my dreams."

1084. Listen to 2,000 hours of positive tapes.

1085. Think of 2,000 ways to be nice.

1086. Think of 2,000 polite words.

1087. Think of 2,000 ways to give thanks.

1088. Say "I love you" 2,000 times.

1089. Say "I'm happy" 2,000 times.

1090. Believe what you say.

1091. Name someone after the M.

1092. Write a list of 2,000 people and things you appreciate.

1093. Tell people 2,000 things you like about them.

1094. Write affirmations on 2,000 pieces of paper and pass them out to people every day.

1095. Write affirmations on 2,000 pieces of paper and read one or more a day to yourself.

1096. Incorporate one positive word in your vocabulary each week.

1097. Begin now to believe in yourself.

1098. If you must preach, then practice what you preach.

1099. Lead by example.

1100. Reward yourself for your good work during the new M.

1101. Make the most out of this new beginning.

1102. You're never too old to jump out of a plane (e.g. George Bush did it!).

1103. Try one new idea a month.

1104. To cherish the past, spend time with a senior citizen.

1105. Think it's too silly? Do it anyway.

1106. Celebrate the successes of others.

1107. Think save and repair, not trash and buy.

1108. Surprise someone with an unexpected visit.

1109. Get a new "do" just for you.

1110. Make time for yourself. You're worth it.

1111. Make an effort to spend less time worrying about things that never happen.

1112. Send a new M telegram to your best friends anywhere.

1113. Start a new M journal.

1114. Go back to school, beginning in the new M.

1115. Don't let life be a soap opera in the next century. Make it an opera!

1116. Make a list of the wishes that come true during the new M.

1117. Make this the year to eliminate one of your fears.

1118. Try to make a difference.

1119. Even if you think you'll fail, you may surprise yourself with success in the new M!

1120. Try something new.

1121. Improve your weaknesses and recognize your strengths in the new M.

1122. Because you can't predict the years left for you, make the most of each one in the new M.

1123. Go to the movies once a month.

1124. Commit to something this year and do it.

1125. Eliminate one mistake every month.

1126. Be on time. Time is precious.

1127. Be thankful every day for what you have.

1128. Be open to new ideas for it's a new M.

1129. If you can't be nice, try not to be mean.

1130. Redefine your life.

1131. Learn about a new culture.

1132. From this point going forward, take a photo of yourself to mark each decade of the rest of your life.

1133. Learn how to use a computer.

1134. Make a difference in someone's life this year.

1135. Stop making excuses. Instead, make it happen.

1136. Do something you used to love and haven't done in a long time.

1137. Call an old flame.

1138. Do what you love.

1139. Love what you do.

1140. This M, do what you know you can do, and don't let others try to dissuade you.

1141. Quit fretting. Start doing. It's a new century.

1142. Make the M full of adventure.

1143. Don't be negative around others.

1144. Every day, find a way to mark the moment.

1145. Mark the moment with style, grace and dignity.

1146. Mark the moment with the people you love.

1147. Mark the moment with new friends.

1148. Take time to sing, dance, love and pray.

1149. Instead of graffiti, discover the art in yourself.

1150. You control your destiny, so start doing what matters most to you!

1151. This year, be happy with what you have.

1152. Be beautiful inside and out. Others will see both sides to you.

1153. Control each day in the M. Don't let your days control you.

1154. Instead of coming up with 2,000 excuses, come up with 2,000 solutions.

1155. Enjoy life's imperfections. They add texture to the years and memories.

1156. Failing is part of life's learning process. Learn from your new M mistakes.

1157. When you encounter someone different than you in the new M, embrace the difference. That's what makes the world unique.

1158. Open closed doors. Look inside. Go inside.

1159. Turn up the tunes when you do the housework this year.

1160. Try as many ideas as you can imagine. One of them will open a door you never imagined!

1161. When something good happens to anyone, congratulate them. What goes around, comes around.

1162. Use what you own.

1163. Share what you have.

1164. Recycle for future generations.

1165. Do something silly this Millennium.

1166. Help make someone else's dream come true.

1167. If you haven't learned to swim yet, do it. Three-fourths of our world is water.

1168. Eliminate 2,000 "nos" from your vocabulary.

1169. Eliminate 2,000 "I can't do that's" from your vocabulary.

1170. Eliminate 2,000 "gripes" from your personality.

1171. Eliminate 2,000 "worries" from your mind.

1172. Eliminate 2,000 "fears" from your heart.

1173. Say "yes" 2,000 times.

1174. Say "I can do that" 2,000 times.

1175. Say "I don't have any gripes" 2,000 times.

1176. Say "I'm not worried" 2,000 times.

1177. Say "I'll risk it" 2,000 times.

Questions

[Note to Our Readers: Why would anyone put questions in a Millennium book? We thought you'd wonder, so here's our explanation: One question can plant a seed that springs to life and rewards you with more pleasure than a dozen roses.]

1178. When's the last time you took a moonlight walk?

1179. When's the last time you smelled a rose?

1180. When's the last time you threw a penny in a wishing well?

1181. When's the last time you wrote a letter to a friend?

1182. When's the last time you had a good conversation?

1183. When's the last time you made time for your family?

1184. When's the last time you made time for your friends?

1185. When's the last time you slept in late?

1186. When's the last time you took a nap?

1187. When's the last time you took an afternoon off?

1188. When's the last time you had a garage sale?

1189. Before you leave your house each day, ask yourself, "Would you really want to know this person?"

1190. Have you ever thought about giving your child a trophy just for being a good kid?

1191. Ever held a ladybug?

1192. Ever clapped your hands to music?

1193. Ever held a lightning bug?

1194. Ever winked at a pretty girl?

1195. Ever smiled with your eyes?

1196. Ever held a baby?

1197. Ever picked up a lucky penny on the sidewalk?

1198. Ever flown a long-tailed kite?

1199. Ever tried skinny dipping?

1200. Ever sampled a foreign food?

1201. Ever smelled honeysuckle on a summer night?

1202. Ever been to an Easter sunrise service?

1203. When's the last time you listened to a book on tape?

1204. When's the last time you heard a choir sing?

1205. When's the last time you read a good book?

1206. Have you ever joined an investment club?

1207. Have you ever created a book club with your friends?

1208. Have you ever entered a contest?

1209. Have you ever taken a continuing education class?

1210. Have you ever gone back to school for another degree?

1211. Have you ever attended a PTA meeting?

1212. Have you ever attended a school board meeting?

1213. Have you ever attended a city council meeting?

1214. If you're not happy with your career, have you ever considered changing it?

1215. Is your child prepared to live in the new M?

1216. Are you prepared to live in the new M?

1217. Are you prepared to celebrate the new M?

1218. Are you prepared to change in the new M?

1219. Are you prepared to find adventure in the new M?

1220. Are you prepared to enjoy the new M?

1221. Are you prepared to try something new in the new M?

1222. Are you prepared to improve yourself in the new M?

1223. Have you created your M license plate?

1224. Have you considered just staying home for New Year's Eve to mark the moment?

1225. If you could have one wish this new M, what would it be?

1226. Can you make a difference in the new M?

1227. How will you make a difference in the new M?

1228. If you could visit one place in the world during the new M, where would it be?

1229. Whatever happened to gut instincts?

1230. When's the last time you worked in the yard together with your kid?

1231. When's the last time you and your kids baked cookies together?

1232. When's the last time you shared a meal together?

1233. When's the last time you made s'mores?

1234. When's the last time you read a bedtime story to your children?

1235. When's the last time you tucked your child into bed and wished your child sweet dreams?

1236. Does the tooth fairy still come to your house?

1237. When's the last time you took your kids to a Dairy Queen?

1238. When's the last time you took your kids to a local lake to feed the ducks?

1239. When's the last time you drove out to the country to enjoy the flowers in the springtime?

1240. When's the last time you drove out to the country to see the leaves changing?

1241. When's the last time you made a snow angel?

1242. When's the last time you had a snowball fight?

1243. When's the last time you made a snowman?

1244. When's the last time you watched a flock of birds migrating?

1245. When's the last time you listened to a night owl?

1246. When's the last time you sat on a porch?

1247. When's the last time you laid out at night to look at the stars and moon?

1248. When's the last time you rocked in a hammock?

1249. When's the last time you went to the circus?

1250. When's the last time you and your family went to the State Fair?

1251. When's the last time you bought popsicles from the ice cream man?

1252. When's the last time you went to a county fair?

1253. When's the last time you left cookies for Santa?

1254. When's the last time you decorated a Christmas tree together?

1255. When's the last time you left an Easter basket at your front door?

1256. When's the last time you went trick or treating with your kids?

1257. When's the last time you celebrated your wedding anniversary?

1258. When's the last time you bought something for your sweetheart, other than flowers or chocolates, on Valentine's Day?

1259. When's the last time your family and relatives have celebrated Thanksgiving together?

1260. When's the last time you called your brother or sister?

1261. When's the last time you called your grandparents?

1262. When's the last time you visited your grandparents?

1263. When's the last time you took your child to a library?

1264. When's the last time you took your child to a ball game?

1265. When's the last time you encouraged your children to talk with you?

1266. When's the last time you explained to your child how to do something right?

1267. When's the last time you thanked your child for a job well done?

1268. When's the last time you hugged your partner?

1269. When's the last time you bought a card for your partner?

1270. When's the last time you sat down to talk with your partner?

1271. When's the last time you left your windows open to feel the fresh air?

1272. When's the last time you had a family meeting?

1273. When's the last time your family went to church together?

1274. When's the last time you prayed together?

1275. When's the last time your family solved family problems together?

1276. When's the last time you said you were sorry to somebody?

1277. When's the last time you said "I love you" and really meant it?

1278. When's the last time you said "thanks" to a teacher, fireman or policeman?

1279. When's the last time you kept your word?

1280. When's the last time you heard a live band?

1281. When's the last time you drove to the beach?

1282. When's the last time you climbed a mountain?

1283. Have you ever seen a desert?

1284. Have you ever seen a shooting star?

1285. Have you ever seen an eclipse?

1286. Have you seen all of our national monuments?

1287. Have you visited all of our national parks?

1288. Have you driven the loneliest highway in America?

1289. Have you climbed Enchanted Rock?

1290. Have you ever been on the Internet?

1291. Have you ever had escargot?

1292. Have you ever had caviar?

1293. Have you ever had country style ribs?

1294. Have you ever had a deep fried turkey?

1295. Have you ever made breakfast over an open fire?

1296. Have you ever spent an evening talking with your neighbors?

1297. Have you ever had a neighborhood cookout?

1298. Have you ever exchanged plants or flowers from your own garden with your neighbors?

1299. Have you ever had a pumpkin carving contest with the kids in your neighborhood?

1300. Have you ever themed your street for any of the holidays?

1301. Have you ever returned to the city where you were born?

1302. Have you ever visited the grave sites of those you loved?

1303. Have you ever competed in amateur sports as an adult?

1304. Do you spend much time doing things together as a couple?

1305. Do you work together on one family project each month?

1306. When's the last time you went Christmas caroling with your family or friends?

1307. Have you ever flown in a plane?

1308. Have you ever been outside your state?

1309. Have you ever adopted a stray dog or cat?

1310. Have you bought a camcorder to record the best moments of your life?

1311. Have you ever tried to find the animals in the clouds?

1312. Have you ever tried to solve a puzzle together?

1313. When's the last time you played checkers?

1314. Have you ever roasted marshmallows over an open fire?

1315. When's the last time you used real logs in your fireplace?

1316. When's the last time you put real butter on your popcorn?

1317. When's the last time you saw the sun's golden carpet on a body of water?

1318. When's the last time you went to a balloon festival?

1319. When's the last time you went to Octoberfest?

1320. When's the last time you went to a tulip festival?

1321. When's the last time you went to a dog parade?

1322. When's the last time you went to an outdoor concert?

1323. When's the last time you sailed on a boat?

1324. Have you ever tried rollerblading?

1325. Have you ever tried flyfishing?

1326. Have you ever tried snowsledding?

1327. Have you ever tried mountain biking?

1328. Have you ever gone skiing hut-to-hut?

1329. Have you ever gone four-wheeling?

1330. Have you ever snowshoed?

1331. Have you ever gone backpacking?

1332. Have you ever ice skated?

1333. Have you ever gone ice fishing?

1334. Have you ever gone snowmobiling?

1335. Have you ever tried cross-country skiing?

1336. Have you ever tried to play the bagpipes?

1337. Have you ever tried to play the harmonica?

1338. Have you ever tried to parasail?

1339. Have you ever been on a hydroplane?

1340. Have you ever crossed a continent?

1341. Have you ever ridden a camel?

1342. Have you ever been to a bat cave?

1343. Have you ever been through an underground cavern?

1344. Have you ever stood on top of a mountain peak?

1345. Have you ever tap danced?

1346. Have you ever gone scuba diving?

1347. Have you ever gone whale watching?

1348. Have you ever been on an Indian reservation?

1349. Have you ever seen buffalo?

1350. Have you ever seen a mountain lion?

1351. Have you ever seen an American eagle?

1352. Have you ever seen salmon swim upstream?

1353. Have you ever seen the changing of the locks at a port?

1354. Have you been to the North or South poles?

1355. How many continents have you visited?

1356. Have you ever seen Spanish moss on a cypress tree?

1357. Have you ever been to New Orleans' Superdome?

1358. Have you ever visited a vineyard?

1359. Have you ever strolled San Antonio's riverwalk?

1360. Have you been to a concert at the Red Rock outdoor amphitheater in Colorado?

1361. Have you seen the hummingbird migration in Chama, New Mexico?

1362. Have you ever toured NASA?

1363. Have you ever walked through the redwood forests of Northern California?

1364. Have you ever experienced Napa, California during harvest season?

1365. Have your feet ever touched the warm, gentle sands of the cool Caribbean?

1366. Have you ever braved the "Hotter than Hell" bike race in Wichita Falls, Texas?

1367. Have you ever tried Fat Tire beer?

1368. Have you ever ridden a bicycle for two?

1369. Have you ever tried doing it yourself versus hiring someone to do it?

1370. When is the last time you rode in a 100-mile bike rally?

1371. When is the last time you walked 100 miles?

1372. When is the last time you went on a spiritual retreat?

1373. Have you ever been to Times Square on New Year's Eve to watch the ball drop at midnight?

1374. Have you ever been to Rockefeller Center to watch the Christmas tree lighting?

1375. Have you ever been to the Tournament of Roses Parade?

1376. Have your eyes ever delighted in the beauty of an English garden?

1377. Have you ever seen the changing of the guards at Buckingham Palace?

1378. Have you ever traveled the Texas highways when the wildflowers are in bloom?

1379. Have you ever dipped into an outdoor spa in the middle of winter?

1380. Have you ever snowskied through an open field in high country?

1381. Ask Bill Gates to invite you to his party. He's booked 1,000 rooms on Fiji.

1382. Spring for the "Le Bal du Roy" dinner and dance at Chateau de Versailles in France for 2,000 euros or about $2,200.

1383. Sign up for New Zealand's January 1, 2000 Millennium Marathon.

1384. Stay on Richard Branson's secluded—and very, very exclusive—island.

1385. Toast the New Year with a pair of Baccarat Millennium glasses.

1386. Buy a bottle of F&F Brunello di Montalcino Riserva 1993, packaged in a 1.5 liter Millennium offering with a miniature fleur-de-lis motif and a silk moir label.

1387. Visit all the countries beginning with "A" the first year of the new M.

1388. Continue with each letter of the alphabet until you've toured the world.

1389. Or visit all the countries beginning with "M" the first year of the new M.

1390. Drop 2,000 flowers over a stadium to celebrate.

1391. Visit the best beaches in the world for the new M.

1392. Charter a sailboat and cruise your favorite isles.

1393. Follow the sunset around the world.

1394. Paint a plane with an M message.

1395. Cruise at high altitudes in your new Cessna.

1396. Go to the championship game of every major sporting event.

1397. Buy your boat this year and go cruising.

1398. Buy your spa this year and just relax in it.

1399. Soak up the rays in a new swimming pool.

1400. Buy a satellite dish to enjoy during the new M.

1401. Crank up the sound in your new home theater system.

1402. Take a plane ride at night with the horizon ahead and toast the sunrise on the new M with champagne.

1403. Buy 2,000 roses for your loved one.

1404. Eat at 2,000 different restaurants.

1405. If you've never really splurged on yourself, do it once in the new M.

1406. Treat yourself to something very fine in the new M.

1407. Treat yourself to something very rare in the new M.

1408. Surf the web on the computer of your dreams.

1409. Design a web page for the new M.

1410. Buy all the tickets to a performance at a 2,000-seat auditorium or stadium.

1411. Blossom in your new greenhouse.

1412. Smell the food on your ultimate grill.

1413. Jump on your new Harley and take the ride of your life.

1414. Rent a ballpark and host a new M softball tournament.

1415. Paint a building with an M message.

1416. Paint a rooftop with an M message.

1417. Attend every major event in the entertainment industry.

1418. Rent a castle for a regal party.

1419. Treat yourself to a Superbowl.

1420. Treat yourself to the Final Four.

1421. Treat yourself to the Olympics in Sydney, Australia.

1422. Treat yourself to the Indy 500.

1423. Treat yourself to the US Open.

1424. Treat yourself to Wimbledon.

1425. Treat yourself to the "Ultimate Millennium Party" at The Premier Hotel in New York. For $3 million, you have the whole hotel to yourself—all 580 guest rooms with meals and beverages.

1426. Treat yourself to the Oscars.

1427. Treat yourself to the Emmys.

1428. Treat yourself to Rio de Janeiro's Samba Festival.

1429. Treat yourself to something wrapped in a Tiffany blue box.

1430. Treat yourself to the MTV Music Awards.

1431. Treat yourself to the Golden Globes.

1432. Treat yourself to the World Cup.

1433. Treat yourself to the Daytona 500.

1434. Treat yourself to the Kentucky Derby.

1435. Treat yourself to the Stanley Cup.

1436. Treat yourself to the World Series.

1437. Treat yourself to the Americas Cup.

1438. Treat yourself to a box of Godiva chocolates.

1439. Buy tickets to Barbara Streisand's M Concert at the MGM Grand in Las Vegas on New Year's Eve. Call 1-800-929-1111 for tickets and room packages.

1440. Travel to an exotic destination every year during the first decade of the M.

1441. Hire a skywriter to write an M message for all to view.

1442. Order the best champagne on the menu.

1443. Order the finest cut of meat on the menu.

1444. Order the most flamboyant dessert on the menu.

1445. Order the best wine on the menu.

1446. Go to Cape Canaveral to watch an actual space shuttle take off.

1447. Install that cozy fireplace you've always wanted in your home.

1448. Hop around the world on the Concorde with Intrav, a St. Louis tour operator, for a mere $75,000!

1449. Visit the NCAA Hall of Champions opening in Indianapolis in spring 2000.

1450. Walk into that high-priced store that you've always passed up and buy something.

1451. Walk into that high-priced restaurant that you've always thought about and dine there.

1452. Rent your dream car for a a night out on the town.

1453. Watch the sun rise and set in all four corners of the U.S.

1454. Grant one new M wish to your employees.

1455. Read 2,000 pages on how successful people reached their goals.

1456. Start a new business by doing what you love and what others say you do well.

1457. Create a new mission statement for the new M.

1458. Organize a Millennium retreat.

1459. Ask for a raise if you haven't received one in a long time. Say something like, "It's been at least a Millennium since my last raise."

1460. Change your uniforms for the new M.

1461. Change your logo for the new M.

1462. Change your letterhead for the new M.

1463. Change your web site for the new M.

1464. Embark on a new M promotional campaign.

1465. Theme your promotions to the new M—make them fresh, fun, and forward-thinking.

1466. Cultivate one new friendship during the new M.

1467. Find a special Millennium mentor for your career.

1468. Arrange a reunion of your office buddies from years past.

1469. Create new M wearables for your company.

1470. Plan your M goals for every 10-year increment.

1471. Celebrate your organization's new M existence.

1472. Develop new M plans for your organization.

1473. Clear out your office of 2,000 sheets of paper.

1474. Recycle those 2,000 sheets of paper.

1475. For your 2,000th customer, give something away.

1476. For your 2,000th phone call, give something away.

1477. Award your top employee a gift certificate for $2,000!

1478. Build a database of 2,000 contacts and prospects for your business.

1479. Have 200 employees write 10 goals each for the new M.

1480. Have 2,000 employees write 1 goal each for the new M.

1481. Give away 2,000 baseballs at the opening home game of the season.

1482. Give away 2,000 miniature footballs at the opening home game of the season.

1483. Get the first toll-free phone number with 2000 in it.

1484. For your 2,000th sale, give something away.

1485. Take a course that you've always put aside for lack of time.

1486. Redesign your office space for the new M.

1487. Paint your storefront with an M message.

1488. Toot your own horn at work during the new M.

1489. Sponsor a community monument or site and dedicate it to the new M.

1490. If you publish a newsletter or magazine, dedicate one issue to the new M.

1491. Send everyone, whose last name begins with "M" in your database, a special Millennium souvenir.

1492. Open a restaurant called "Food for the M."

1493. At theme parks, create special M rides.

1494. Set up a web site to trade Millennium memorabilia.

1495. Print an M label for your letters and packages.

1496. Announce your M news with a billboard.

1497. Name a product after the Millennium.

1498. Rent a billboard and put up your favorite message. Photograph it for a keepsake!

1499. Make your computer(s) Y2K bug-free.

1500. Announce your M projects with a billboard.

1501. Announce your M news in the paper.

1502. Announce your M news on the radio.

1503. Sponsor an M ideas contest on the radio.

1504. Sponsor an M ideas contest with your newspaper.

1505. Sponsor Y2K radio contests.

1506. Sponsor Y2K TV shows.

1507. Start an M newsletter online.

1508. Theme your sales incentives and awards around the M.

1509. Create an M hanging mobile for your office.

1510. Open an M savings account.

1511. Patent something during the first year of the new M.

1512. Set M goals that you can accomplish each month, quarter, and year.

1513. Create an employee contest to find the best ways to improve your business in the new M.

1514. Form an M chat group.

1515. Celebrate your company's birthday lavishly in the first year of the new M.

1516. Take a picture of your entire team, division or company in the first year of the new M.

1517. Create a Millennium sales contest.

1518. Sponsor a Millennium think tank.

1519. Check out Fidelity Investment's new M Mutual Fund (rated among the Top 25 Growth Funds by Investor's Business Daily).

1520. Offer your employees training to improve their skills for the new M.

1521. Theme an event for the new M that raises needed funds for an important purpose.

1522. Paint your delivery truck with a new M logo and motto.

1523. Stay out of the way of someone who makes things happen in the new M.

1524. Have a new M company birthday party, themed with Year 2000 souvenirs.

1525. Create an M-named sports team.

1526. Create an M-inspired slogan for your team.

1527. Create an M-themed t-shirt for your team.

1528. Photograph your M team for the record.

1529. Send your M team photo to your local paper for the record.

1530. Create an M page for your web site.

1531. Link to other M web sites.

1532. If everything crashes because of Y2K, just chill out, walk out, and enjoy the way the world is.

1533. Seize this opportunity to change your company culture, vision, and message if it will raise you to the next level of success.

1534. Seize this opportunity to do good for your community.

1535. Adopt a memorable and significant cause or project.

1536. Start an M newsletter to announce your good news.

1537. Create a sales contest tied to any number beginning with 2 (e.g. $2,000 in sales; $20,000 in sales; $200,000 in sales, etc.).

1538. Send out 2,000 direct mail pieces to promote your product or service. (Buy a good mailing list!)

Goalsetting 15

[A Note to Our Readers: Yes, we know how hard it is to set and keep goals. But we had to include this chapter. Afterall, how can you begin a new Millennium without at least one goal?]

1539. Set a goal of listing 2,000 positive things about yourself.

1540. Set a goal of listing 2,000 positive things about your spouse.

1541. Set a goal of giving yourself a pat on the back every day for the next 2,000 days.

1542. Set a goal of knowing what you really want by a certain day in the new M.

1543. List 2,000 things you really want and narrow your list down to the top 100.

1544. Accomplish at least 10 of these goals each year for the next century.

1545. Set a goal of giving 2,000 people a sincere compliment.

1546. Set a goal of saving $2 a day for 2,000 days.

1547. Set a goal of not smoking for 2,000 minutes.

1548. Set a goal of raising $2,000 for an important project in your community.

1549. Set a community goal of raising $2,000,000 to fund a major improvement in your home town.

1550. Set a goal of running 2,000 miles during the first year of the new M.

1551. Set a goal of biking 2,000 miles during the first year of the new M.

1552. Set a goal of saving $2,000 during the first year of the new M.

1553. Set a goal of walking 2,000 miles during the first year of the new M.

1554. Set a goal of saying 2,000 prayers during the first year of the new M.

1555. Set a goal of planting 2,000 trees during the new M.

1556. Set a goal of donating 2,000 items to a good cause during the new M.

1557. Set a personal goal.

1558. Set a business goal.

1559. Set a small goal.

1560. Set a big goal.

1561. Set a distant goal.

1562. Complete several of these goals during the first year of the new M.

1563. Buy that one, overpriced sports memento.

1564. Buy that one, overpriced sports car.

1565. Buy that one, overpriced ring.

1566. Buy that one, overpriced watch.

1567. Take that one, overpriced cruise.

1568. Take that one, overpriced vacation.

1569. Buy the best seat in the house for your favorite sports event.

1570. Buy the best seat in the house for your favorite opera.

1571. Buy the best seat in the house for your favorite concert.

1572. Buy the best seat in the house for your favorite play.

1573. Treat yourself to that one, overpriced but memorable meal out.

1574. Stay at a romantic bed and breakfast.

1575. Reserve a movie theater for you and your friends.

1576. Reserve a roller rink for you and your friends.

1577. Reserve your favorite pub for a party.

1578. Reserve your favorite city swimming pool for a private pool party.

1579. Ride a trolley.

1580. Fly away to a romantic place for dinner and dancing.

1581. Fly first-class.

1582. Take the Orient Express.

For Texas Wannabes

[A Note to Our Readers: We couldn't resist throwing in a few ideas here. Since Annemarie is a native Texan, she just had to brag about her Lone Star State!]

1583. Rent a ranch for the night and two-step the new M away!

1584. Go two-stepping in pair of Lucchese 2000 boots.

1585. Serve up 2,000 pounds of barbecue in your Texas-sized backyard and be sure you've stocked 2,000 ice, cold longnecks, too!

1586. Buy all the tickets to a night at the rodeo and invite your friends.

1587. Rent a Country Western dance hall and hire a great band from Austin to perform.

1588. Give away Stetsons to mark the moment.

1589. Set up a group camp under a starry Texas sky.

1590. Sponsor a non-stop Country Western dance marathon that runs at least 2,000 minutes.

1591. Ask your local DJ to play the top 2,000 Country Western songs of all time.

1592. Criss-cross 2,000 miles of Texas to explore its unique and varied character.

1593. Spend the night in the Fort Worth Stockyards Hotel and reminisce about the Wild West and other tall tales while you're kicking back in the saloon.

Environmental

[A Note to Our Readers: Debbie loves the outdoors, and Annemarie marched on the first Earth Day. So we were compelled to present these Millennium ideas to you. Wouldn't the world be happier if we shared more green space together?]

1594. Spend 2,000 minutes outside enjoying nature.

1595. Learn the names of 2,000 stars.

1596. Donate 2,000 seedlings to a local park.

1597. Put together 2,000 bags of birdseed, and pass them out to everybody.

1598. Try to spot 2,000 birds during the Year 2000.

1599. Release 2,000 lady bugs in an open field.

1600. Release 2,000 fireflies in an open field at dusk.

1601. Release 2,000 earthworms in a community garden.

1602. Gather 2,000 pieces of trash off the beach.

1603. Recycle 2,000 bottles, cans, or newspapers.

1604. Throw 2,000 flower seeds in an open field.

1605. Plant a field of flowers to celebrate.

1606. Plant a tree to celebrate.

1607. Plant a garden to celebrate.

1608. Plant a grove of trees to celebrate.

1609. Line your street with trees to celebrate.

1610. Watch a flower bloom.

1611. Look at the sky every day. It's a constantly changing canvas.

1612. Make one improvement to your favorite park.

1613. Visit the nation's top 10 best-kept public lawns during the M. (Voted tops by lawn experts in random order: 1) Cypress Gardens, 2) Bayou Bend Collection and Gardens, 3) Middleton Place Gardens, 4) Central Park, 5) Brookfield Zoo, 6) Margaret Mitchell House & Museum, 7) Field of Dreams Movie Site, 8) Graceland, 9) Rose Bowl, and 10) Daytona International Speedway Infield.

1614. Begin to recycle this M.

1615. Adopt a lake.

1616. Adopt a city park.

1617. Adopt a street.

1618. Have a trash bash to collect at least 2,000 pieces of litter.

1619. If you don't have trees in your yard, plant one.

1620. If you don't have flowers in your yard, plant some.

1621. If you've never done a big spring cleaning, do it now.

1622. If there's an older neighbor who needs help in the yard, lend a helping hand.

1623. Buy a migratory map and follow the paths of birds in migration.

1624. Buy a telescope, binoculars, or microscope to see something new.

1625. Become involved in saving something that is almost extinct.

1626. Become involved in taking something off the endangered species list.

1627. Get an M Earth MasterCard. (Note: A minimum of $200,000 will be donated to non-profit organizations through the M 2000 Project.)

1628. Try to find a 2,000-year-old tree in your community and dedicate it with a plaque.

1629. Search for a 2,000-year-old fossil or artifact.

1630. Visit a museum with a 2,000-year-old fossil or artifact.

1631. Find a bare parcel of land in your community and lay down 2,000 pieces of sod.

1632. Watch the birds build their nests in the spring.

1633. Take your family for a picnic at the park.

1634. Leave animals that belong in nature alone. Let them party, too.

1635. Visit your local botanical gardens or arboretum.

1636. Watch the hummingbird migration in the fall in Rockport, Texas.

1637. Hold a housewarming party and invite everyone to bring one plant to landscape your yard.

1638. Buy a bird feeder instead of a bird cage.

1639. Create more green space.

1640. Buy pens that refill.

1641. Buy razors that refill.

1642. Dedicate a new M park in your community.

1643. Create an oasis in your own backyard.

1644. If you have trees, hire a good arborist to keep them healthy.

1645. If your city has a tired spot, beautify it.

1646. If you spot litter in your state, pick it up.

1647. While you're visiting a national park, ask what you can do while you're there.

1648. When touring a foreign country, leave it in better condition than when you visited.

1649. Recycle 2,000 soft drink cans.

1650. Recycle 2,000 plastic jugs.

1651. Recycle 2,000 glass bottles.

1652. Bring your own shopping bag.

1653. Compost.

1654. Hang your clothes out to dry.

1655. Fix it.

1656. Plant hope.

1657. Shower happiness.

1658. Dig good deeds.

1659. Cultivate friendships.

1660. Grow old happily.

[A Note to Our Readers: Okay, we admit that we left out a few states. Maybe our steam was running out? Feel free to brainstorm ways to celebrate your own home state here.]

1661. If you're from Hawaii, send 2,000 leis to your friends.

1662. If you're from Georgia, give away 2,000 bags of peanuts.

1663. If you're from Florida, send 2,000 oranges to your neighbors.

1664. If you're from Texas, buy boots for 2,000 of your best buddies.

1665. If you're from Virginia, give away 2,000 Virginia hams.

1666. If you're from Arizona, hand out 2,000 vials of colored sand.

1667. If you're from New York, send out 2,000 big apples.

1668. If you're from Nevada, send out 2,000 poker chips. (Check out www.2000nevada.com for Nevada's Millennium Magic events!)

1669. If you're from Colorado, give out 2,000 pine cones.

1670. If you're from New Mexico, send out 2,000 strings of chili peppers.

1671. If you're from California, give away 2,000 boxes of raisins with the message: "Raisin' Hell during the Millennium."

1672. If you're from Michigan, pass out 2,000 hood ornaments.

1673. If you're from Vermont, send out 2,000 gallons of maple syrup.

1674. If you're from Alaska, have a hut building contest with 2,000 bricks of ice.

1675. If you're from Arkansas, enlist 2,000 contestants for a razor back hog calling contest.

1676. If you're from Connecticut, give out 2,000 copies of the U.S. Constitution.

1677. If you're from Delaware, give a diamond to your loved one.

1678. If you're from Idaho, have a 2,000 pound potato mashing contest.

1679. If you're from Indiana, have a 2,000 free throws contest.

1680. If you're from Iowa, have a 2,000 ear corn shucking contest.

1681. If you're from Illinois, send out 2,000 log cabin kits.

1682. If you're from Kansas, sponsor an essay contest explaining why "There's no place like home."

1683. If you're from Kentucky, bet 2,000 pennies on the prettiest horse.

1684. If you're from Louisiana, catch and boil 2,000 crawfish.

1685. If you're from Maine, hold a 2,000 pound lobster party.

1686. If you're from Minnesota, visit 2,000 of its 10,000 lakes.

1687. If you're from Mississippi, beautify a major boulevard with 2,000 magnolia trees.

1688. If you're from Montana, have a Montana Millennium Rodeo.

1689. If you're from New Jersey, take a 2,000 mile hike into nature.

1690. If you're from North Dakota, send 2,000 sunflower seeds to all your buddies.

1691. If you're from Tennessee, hold a new M country songwriting contest.

1692. If you're from Washington, D.C., relive the first Millennium at the Smithsonian Institute.

1693. If you're from Wisconsin, send out 2,000 pounds of cheddar cheese.

1694. If you're from Wyoming, kiss 2,000 cowboys.

1695. Blow your car horn on January 1, 2000.

1696. Decorate your car with a new M theme.

1697. Write "Honk for Y2K" on your car.

1698. Then, ask your neighbors to do these things, too.

1699. Build a house that will be ready for move-in on the first day of the new M.

1700. Start your own business on the first day of the new M.

1701. Announce a new product line on the first day of the new M.

1702. Meet someone new on the first day of the new M.

1703. Do something you've never done before on the first day of the new M.

1704. Watch the sun rise and the sun set on the first day of the new M.

1705. Yell "Happy M!" on the first day.

1706. Get baptized.

1707. Have your baby.

1708. Just enjoy the first day of the new M.

1709. On the first day of the new M, think about all the good things you've accomplished in the last M.

1710. On the first day of the new M, think of all the opportunities that lie ahead.

1711. Record where you are and what you do on the first day.

1712. Take a family photo on the first day, then 5 years later, and 10 years later. Treasure these photos.

1713. Keep track of your entire first M year.

1714. Drink mimosas at sunrise and margaritas at sunset.

1715. Record the first day of the M on film or video or digital camera.

1716. Buy a newspaper from your local community on the first day of the M.

1717. Pass out kazoos to your neighbors and blow them all day long.

1718. Put out new M yard signs to celebrate. Make extras for your neighbors, too.

1719. Rescue a good friend from being alone on the first day of the M.

1720. Spend the first day of the M watching sci-fi movies.

1721. Sleep in on the first day of the M.

1722. Call all of your family the first day, and wish everyone a "Happy new M!"

1723. Collect newspapers from a major city in every state on the first day of the new M.

1724. If you're building something, imprint your hand or foot or message to mark the first day of the M.

1725. Have your palm read on the first day of the M.

1726. Have your fortune told on the first day of the M.

1727. Save some champagne for mimosas on the first day of the M.

1728. Do something unique on the first day of the M.

1729. Don't commit to anything on the first day of the M.

1730. Design a special insert for your local paper.

1731. Distribute miniature M flags in everyone's front yard.

1732. Have a new M yard decorating contest for the first day.

1733. Have an M block party on the first day.

1734. Sponsor a gala fireworks display for your community.

1735. Rent a plane with a banner trailer to promote your new M message.

1736. Ask someone to marry you.

1737. Attend a sunrise service.

1738. Coordinate a horn blowing with all your neighbors on January 1, 2000.

1739. Tie helium balloons to every street sign in your neighborhood to celebrate the M.

1740. Tie ribbons on every tree to celebrate the M in your neighborhood.

1741. Throw a tailgate party in your driveway and invite all your neighbors to join you.

1742. Set up your grill in your front yard and invite your neighbors over to celebrate.

1743. Get involved in your neighborhood.

1744. Form an M investment club.

1745. Have a front yard get together every month with your neighbors.

1746. Spell out the word "millennium" with all your neighbors.

1747. Take an aerial photograph of this "living" word.

1748. Befriend a senior citizen in your neighborhood.

1749. Know your neighborhood police patrol.

1750. Show your kids the neighborhood where you grew up.

1751. Take a stroll through your neighborhood.

1752. Host an outdoor grill fest in your local park for 2,000 people.

1753. Release 2,000 butterflies at your neighborhood park.

1754. Get your neighborhood to light up your street with outdoor lights.

1755. Walk through a different part of your neighborhood once a month.

1756. Get to know your neighbors.

1757. Create an M parade for your neighborhood.

1758. Create an M play day with clowns, balloons, and a petting zoo for the kids in your neighborhood.

1759. Adopt a community project to help clean up your neighborhood.

1760. Make one improvement to your neighborhood.

1761. Visit a neighborhood you've never seen. Begin now to create understanding among all who live within your community.

1762. Give away $2,000 in trees to beautify your neighborhood.

1763. Give away $2,000 in exercise equipment to your neighborhood recreation center.

1764. Ask your local coffee house to package a special blend of coffee and label it "New M Brew."

1765. Create your own Millennium label for your homemade treats.

1766. If you really want to be clever, go to a wine store and look for a label that matches your name or your company's name—some do! Then order a bottle for every client and send these along with a wonderful Millennium note.

1767. Send out 2,000 packages of mint gum with this message: "Hope the Millennium brings you a mint of success."

1768. Imprint 2,000 balloons with the saying, "Make it a blow out in the new M."

1769. Give away 2,000 bags of popcorn with the M motto, "Hope the new M is popping with fun!"

1770. Give away 2,000 rubber balls with the motto, "Have a ball in the new M."

1771. Give out 2,000 yardsticks with a motto about "measuring up in the new M."

1772. Imprint 2,000 new M sunglasses.

1773. Give away helium balloons filled with new M messages as party favors.

1774. Find something in an antique store or flea market from the past M and buy it.

1775. Set aside something that you want to pass down to your kids for the new M.

1776. Save a newspaper or magazine that comes out at the start of each decade for the new M.

1777. Collect the commemorative stamps of the last M.

1778. Design an M remembrance ring.

1779. Design an M remembrance necklace.

1780. Design an M commemorative coin.

1781. Design an M commemorative plaque.

1782. Create an M bandanna.

1783. Create an M Frisbee.

1784. Create an M word bracelet.

1785. Create an M word necklace.

1786. Create an M-flavored ice cream.

1787. Design a new M sunshade.

1788. Order personalized new M license plates.

1789. Collect stories from people about the craziest things that happened to them during the first year of the new M and write a book about them.

1790. Design an M screensaver.

1791. Create a Millennium tool belt with high tech gadgets.

1792. Imprint 2,000 pens or pencils with the message: "Pencil me in to celebrate the new M with you!"

1793. Design a new M t-shirt with your favorite new century motto. Wear it and share it!

1794. Check out the M stationery from Idea Art at 1-800-433-2278.

1795. Create an M parade for your town.

1796. Create a hybrid rose for the M.

1797. Buy every bottle of wine beginning with an "M" and start your new M wine collection.

1798. Design an M hot air balloon.

1799. Design an M mousepad.

1800. Design an M keyboard.

1801. Design an M picture frame.

1802. Design an M wallpaper.

1803. Design an M welcome mat.

1804. Design an M party favor.

1805. Design an M doll.

1806. Design an M newsletter.

1807. Create a M bookmark.

1808. Design a new M lapel pin.

1809. Create a new M lipstick.

1810. Create a new M cereal.

1811. Create a new M billboard.

1812. Create an M ballcap.

1813. Use this slogan: "Make it happen in Y2K."

1814. Use this slogan: "Who cares about Y2K?"

1815. Use this slogan: "Beach it in Y2K"

1816. Use this slogan: "What's Y2K?"

1817. Use this slogan: "FCKY2K"

1818. Use this slogan: "Play in Y2K"

1819. Use this slogan: "I Matter in the new M."

1820. Use this slogan: "Ready for the new M?"

1821. Use this slogan: "The new M rocks!"

1822. Use this slogan: "Embrace the new M."

1823. Create a Y2K survival kit.

1824. Create a Y2K "how to" check list.

1825. Create a t-shirt using this slogan: "I Survived Y2K."

1826. Create a t-shirt using this slogan: "We made it to Y2K."

1827. Create a commemorative M label, carton, or bag.

1828. Package a commemorative M tea.

1829. Bottle a commemorative M beer.

1830. Bottle a commemorative M wine.

1831. Bottle a commemorative M champagne.

1832. Create a magic wand for those who want their dreams to come true in the new M.

1833. Ask your florist to create an M flower arrangement.

1834. Create a miniature M flag for your car's antennae.

1835. Design an M trash bag, because you know what it will be like after the party's over!

1836. Get an M tattoo.

1837. Design a new hairdo for the M.

1838. Paint your face with an M design.

1839. Mow the number 2,000 in your yard.

1840. Have the barber write the number 2,000 on the back of your head.

1841. Make a sculpture out of 2,000 toothpicks.

1842. Trim your shrubs into the number 2,000.

1843. Wallpaper your room with 2s and 0s.

1844. Bake a 2,000 pound M cake.

1845. Throw a Martian and Martini party.

1846. Throw a Star Wars party.

1847. Have your party catered by aliens.

1848. Make a 2,000 foot long M sandwich.

1849. Sculpt a 2,000 pound M ice sculpture.

1850. Party with Mike, the M Party Animal. Call 1-800-365-9360 for details.

1851. Organize the next Woodstock for the new M.

1852. Paint your fingernails with a new M message.

1853. Rent your local zoo and throw an Animal House party.

1854. Pitch a tent on a beach for a month.

1855. Enjoy a 2,000 minute massage.

1856. Play musical chairs with 2,000 people.

1857. Deliver 2,000 pizzas with the Year 2000 spelled on them in pepperoni.

1858. Have a Millennium shoe party. Ask your friends to decorate a pair of shoes with a futuristic look.

1859. Give someone a bouquet of pinwheels.

1860. Paint your toe nails with a new M message like "Happy New YR."

1861. Visit every state that starts with an "M."

1862. Visit every major city that starts with an "M."

1863. Visit every country that starts with an "M."

1864. Sit on a park bench and watch everyone else celebrate the new M.

1865. Watch the news for 24-hours on the first day of the M.

1866. Set up an M juice and beverage stand (e.g. mango, mimosa, mocha).

1867. Decorate your home with chairs from each decade of the past M.

1868. Instead of dieting, the first week of the M, eat ALL of your favorite foods!

1869. Paint the bumpers of your car with a new M message.

1870. Throw a new M costume party and invite your guests to come as their favorite aliens.

1871. Name someone after the M.

1872. Paint a brick wall with an M collage.

1873. Write an M message on the roof of your house.

1874. Write an M message in the sand on the beach.

1875. Create a kazoo band for the new M. Perform in public!

1876. Say to yourself 2,000 times, "I'll never ever drink as much as I did on December 31, 1999."

Party On!

[Note to Our Readers: Just want to party? Then, these ideas will add spice to your life. From the simple to the ridiculous, why not try something different in the new M?]

1877. Party for a full 24 hours!

1878. Blow your car horn on January 1, 2000.

1879. Sponsor a surfing contest with 2,000 entries.

1880. Paint your car or truck with an M message.

1881. Paint the front windows of your home with an M message.

1882. Throw an M "tux and gown" party with turn-of-the-century clothing.

1883. Develop a recipe for your own M party cocktail.

1884. Rent a giant inflatable balloon for your party.

1885. Don't let anything balloon out of proportion in the new M!

1886. Celebrate living to the new M.

1887. Blindfold a friend and drive him or her to a special place to celebrate.

1888. Hire a band for your backyard party.

1889. Have an M painting party to spruce up a room in your home.

1890. Rent a bus and bring your best friends along to travel 2,000 miles of California highways, byways and vineyards.

1891. Throw a wine tasting party featuring 2,000 of California's best cabernets, chardonnays, and champagnes.

1892. Order a cake with the number "2000" spelled on it and celebrate!

1893. Stage a hand-holding sit-in at Golden Gate Park to welcome the new M.

1894. Decorate with 2,000 helium balloons and release them at once.

1895. Rent a speed boat for a weekend trip.

1896. Rent a houseboat for a party with your friends.

1897. Write your problems, worries, or concerns on pieces of paper and release them in helium balloons.

1898. Throw a costume new M party where people dress as their favorite heroes and heroines.

1899. Celebrate and welcome the new M by counting down on your computer.

1900. Watch 2001: A Space Odyssey.

1901. Theme your sports event around the M.

1902. Theme your big party for the year around the M.

1903. Throw an M slumber party.

1904. Celebrate your birthday, promotion, or retirement in M style.

1905. Have an M day at the ballpark.

1906. Theme your bachelor party for the M.

1907. Theme a party from an era of the past M.

1908. Have a new M reflection party.

1909. Have an M countdown party.

1910. Check out the SAM Millennium II ball machine from Master Sports. Call 1-800-837-1002 or visit their web sit at www.mastersports.com

1911. Give away 2,000 party horns.

1912. Make predictions for the new M with your friends, then get together a year later to see which ones came true.

1913. Blow 2,000 bubbles in an open field.

1914. Give away 2,000 kazoos to celebrate.

1915. Create a kazoo band for the new M. Perform in public!

1916. Light 2,000 candles and turn off the lights to enjoy.

1917. Make up a new M dance.

1918. Pick a beautiful new M day and hit the road in a convertible.

1919. Have a romantic dinner under a full Millennium moon.

Creative Concepts

[A Note to Our Readers: Need fresh ideas? Try these to celebrate the new M.]

1920. Create an M collage of all your dreams.

1921. Create an M collage of all your hopes.

1922. Create an M collage of all your friends.

1923. Create an M collage of all your family.

1924. Create an M collage of your favorite hobbies.

1925. Create an M collage of your favorite heroes and heroines.

1926. Create an M collage of all your mentors.

1927. Create an M collage of all your travels.

1928. Create an M collage of all your favorite sports.

1929. Create an M collage of all your favorite adventures.

1930. Create an M collage of all your accomplishments.

1931. Create an M collage of all your favorite musicians.

1932. Compose an M song.

1933. Write an M play.

1934. Write an M book.

1935. Write an M prayer.

1936. Draw an M picture.

1937. Create an M line dance.

1938. Design a pair of M sunglasses.

1939. Create an M menu for a restaurant.

1940. Design a new M bumper sticker.

1941. Create an M gift basket.

1942. Sponsor a new M kite design competition.

1943. Design an M treasure hunt.

1944. Create an M trivia game.

1945. Create an M cybergame.

1946. Create a new M word.

1947. Design a new M quilt pattern.

1948. Create a new M line of greeting cards.

1949. Create a new M calendar of your favorite moments.

1950. Design a special piece of new M jewelry for someone dear to you.

1951. Design a commemorative new M plate.

1952. Design a commemorative Christmas ornament.

1953. Design an M stamp.

1954. Create a wall of new M quotes.

1955. Create a miniature M flag for your car's antennae.

1956. Start an M novel online and solicit the world's contributions.

1957. Ask your florist to create an M flower arrangement.

[A Note to Our Readers: Do you really want to pay the exorbitant prices for travel during the eve of the Millennium? Why not wait a month—or, better yet, a year to take your special trip. In the meantime, consider these fun alternatives.]

1958. Skip work and rent a convertible on the first beautiful day of the new M.

1959. Fly 2,000 miles in a hot air balloon.

1960. Plan your dream vacation for the first year of the new M.

1961. Explore 2,000 miles of coast line.

1962. See the first leaves change in New England in the new M.

1963. If you've never been to the opening ceremonies of the National Baseball League, get there this year.

1964. Follow a rainbow from end to end.

1965. Go to Mardi Gras.

1966. If you've never been to NASA, go visit it and think about the travels of the new M.

1967. Watch the U.S. bring home America's Cup in 2000. Get details at www.ac2000.org.

1968. Celebrate the opening of The Women's Museum which will open in October 2000 in Dallas, Texas as the most comprehensive women's history museum in the U.S. Check out the web site at www.thewomensmuseum.org

1969. Go to a planetarium to celebrate the M.

1970. Camp at Napa Valley State Park during harvest season.

1971. Take a moonlight cruise.

1972. Take time off to travel Route 66.

1973. Indulge in Ten Thousand Waves in Santa Fe, New Mexico.

1974. Tour all the monuments in Washington, DC.

1975. Visit Plymouth Rock.

1976. Look up an item in history for every century preceding the Year 2000.

1977. Travel an historical trail during the new M.

1978. Visit the historical churches throughout the U.S. on a special M tour.

1979. Go see the Northern Lights.

1980. Travel to Alaska's great frontier.

1981. Watch the sun set in Hawaii.

1982. Watch the sun rise in the Virgin Islands.

1983. Watch the moon rise over Mt. Olympus.

[A Note to Our Readers: We're really flower kids at heart. For the spiritual side of your new M experience, let these thoughts flow through you by reading and repeating them.]

1984. Be happy.
Seek peace.
Find prosperity.

1985. Be happy with yourself.
Seek peace within yourself.
Find prosperity from within.

1986. Be happy with what you have.
Seek peace with others.
Find prosperity with your talents.

1987. Be happy for those who succeed.
Seek peace when you are most fearful.
Find prosperity by wishing others well.

1988. Be happy with your life.
Seek peace through friendship.
Find prosperity through diligence.

1989. Be happy when it's sunny.
Be happy when it's raining.
Be happy that you're alive.

1990. Seek peace within yourself.
Wish peace for others.
Promote world peace.

1991. Find prosperity in your home.
Find prosperity in your work.
Find prosperity in your friendships.

1992. Before you judge, listen.

1993. Before you take, give.

1994. Before you give up, try again.

1995. Before you despair, pray.

1996. Before you blame, ask.

1997. Before you leap, look.

1998. Before you ignore, explore.

1999. Before you criticize, empathize.

2000. Let these ideas spark new ones for you. Mark the moment! Happy Millennium!